LORD HEL

MW00789161

SEEK THE Precious Moments

Becky Blackmon

Publishing Designs, Inc.
Huntsville, Alabama

Publishing Designs, Inc.
P.O. Box 3241
Huntsville, Alabama 35810

© 2019 Becky Blackmon
Second printing, June 2021

Cover and Text Design: Crosslin Creative.net

Images: Shutterstock, Dollarphotoclub.com

Editors: Peggy Coulter and Debra G. Wright

Printed in the United States of America

Publisher's Cataloging in Publication Data

Blackmon, Becky 1948—

Seek the Precious Moments / Becky Blackmon

252 pp.

13 chapters and study questions

1. Spiritual Priorities—Women. 2. Time Management Obstacles 3. Parenting against Satan

I. Title.

ISBN 978-1-945127-14-4

248.8

Dedication

To my Father in heaven who has always found the time for me and who has been so compassionate, long suffering, and merciful while I was finding the time for Him.

Also, to Phil and Cathy Hudson, my brother and sister in Christ, who so graciously surrounded me with their unconditional love and a heavenly place to work. You truly are "cold water to a weary soul" (Proverbs 25:25). You both made this book possible. Thank you for loving me.

Acknowledgments

Thanks to my precious family for loving me with true agape love and finding the time for me. There simply are not enough words to express how much I love and adore you. My cup runs over with love.

And thank you, my sisters, whom I have asked to pray for me and this book. I love all of you with all my heart. Thank you for your prayers and for loving the Lord and me.

Thank you, Peggy Coulter, for believing in me and encouraging me beyond words. You are truly my Barnabas.

And last of all, thank you, my precious Liz, for picking up where Mama left off.

Endorsements

Becky contrasts, "running, running like a hamster on its crazy spinning wheel" with "be still and know that I am God." She encourages, "Immerse yourself in pleasing Him. Let your world revolve around your Father."

—Brenda Birckholtz, contributing author of *Mentor Me*

A book full of practical pearls of truth that get down to where we live . . . a commentary on God's admonition to redeem the time. Pulsating with spiritual emotion . . . it promotes self-reflection. Select a quiet place and let this book help to draw you near to the heart of God.

—Frank Chesser, author of *Portrait of God* and others

"Time with Becky" shares experiences that grab your attention and open your heart. Each chapter causes you to ponder and appreciate that precious moments in life are times with God.

—Cynthia Guy, author of *Sweet Truths, Journey to a Better Place*, and others

Seek the Precious Moments is as real as it gets. You may laugh and cry as Becky describes life as we know it and shows us how to find peace and purpose in the midst of it all.

—Kathy Pollard, author of *Return to Me*

Becky reminds us of the necessity of regularly examining our personal priorities alongside God's will. We will not accidentally stumble on these precious moments. We must actively seek them.

—Kathy McWhorter Kendall, author of *A Chosen Few*

Becky Blackmon reaches into life's rapid pace and snatches us back into reality to remind us to stop and take time to enjoy the aroma of God's precious roses. Inspiring!

—Scott Harp, website editor, TheRestorationMovement.com, Russell-ville, Kentucky

Seek the Precious Moments will make you feel as though you are sitting at Becky's feet listening to her teach. Her "Pause and Ponder" and "Keep Seeking" questions encourage thoughtful application of God's will.

—Dwina W. Willis, associate professor, retired

This book will capture your attention, even after you put it down. I would read a chapter in the morning, and then find myself revisiting the thoughts, lessons, and poignant stories throughout the day. In *Seek the Precious Moments*, Becky opens up her heart of wisdom, and invites us in to get a healthy share. Her writing is funny at times, convicting at others, but one thing it is not is ambiguous. Becky takes a firm and clear stand on the truth of God's Word. Oh how we need it!

—Celine Sparks, author of *How to Train Your Dragon* and others

Contents

Introduction

Lord, Help Me

As they were going along the road, someone said to Him, "I will follow You wherever You go." And Jesus said to him, "The foxes have holes and the birds of the air have nests, but the Son of Man has nowhere to lay His head." And He said to another, "Follow Me." But he said, "Lord, permit me first to go and bury my father." But He said to him, "Allow the dead to bury their own dead; but as for you, go and proclaim everywhere the kingdom of God." Another also said, "I will follow You, Lord; but first permit me to say good-bye to those at home." But Jesus said to him, "No one, after putting his hand to the plow and looking back, is fit for the kingdom of God" (Luke 9:57–62).

But some days later Felix arrived with Drusilla, his wife who was a Jewess, and sent for Paul and heard him speak about faith in Christ Jesus. But as he was discussing righteousness, self-control and the judgment to come, Felix became frightened and said, "Go away for the present, and when I find time I will summon you" (Acts 24:24–25).

"Behold, I stand at the door and knock; if anyone hears My voice and opens the door, I will come in to him and will dine with him, and he with Me" (Revelation 3:20).

Seek the Precious Moments

The Master of the universe, the Son of God, the Shepherd of us all beckons us to follow Him. He stands at the door of our hearts and kindly invites us to open the door and let Him into our lives.

What will it be, my sisters? Will we grant Jesus access to our moments, our homes, and our hearts? Do we have time for the "Lamb of God who takes away the sins of the world"? Do we seek moments for the blood-covered Savior who died for us on an old rugged cross?

The bottom line question of yesterday, today, and tomorrow is this: Will we find the time for Jesus?

Before we begin this study together, I must say thank you to the readers. Please take your time and don't rush through it. Be sure to read "Time with Becky" before each chapter. Pause, think, peruse, and consider. These moments are especially from me to you—from my heart to yours. Take the time . . . and always remember that I love you and that I am praying for you.

Becky

"There is more to life than increasing its speed."

—Mahatma Gandhi

"Oh dear! Oh dear! I shall be too late!"

—The Rabbit, *Alice's Adventures in Wonderland* by Lewis Carroll

Hurry, Hurry, Hurry!

My mom was naturally funny—sometimes hysterical. Not only could Mom find humor in all she attempted, but she sure had a way of describing a simple life experience (and re-enacting it) to the point that you, the listener, found yourself somehow on the floor, holding your sides, laughing, and begging, "Stop! Stop!"

Mom was quite the verbal artist. She had the extraordinary gift of painting an exact picture of a seemingly ordinary event, drawing you into the middle of it, and then showing you the absurdity of it all. You, the listener, soon realized that you too had probably had a million of those hysterical moments yourself but never perceived it, that is, until Lea Fowler described one moment from her own life.

Our family adored these stories she told over and over, and we all had our favorites.

"Hey, Mom, tell the story about the time you were a teenager and didn't know how to drive a car but drove your daddy's car anyway!" (and wrecked it).

"Hey, Ticky," (her name dubbed by her grandchildren), "tell about the time Uncle Tom and Mama locked you in the gas station's bathroom on purpose while on a family vacation?"

"Hey, Mom, tell about that time again when we were kids in Oklahoma and it was snowy and icy. Daddy tied a rope on the back of the car and to our sled, and we rode the back roads and hung on for dear life." We kids thought it was great— today it would be called child abuse and a seven-year prison sentence.

"Tell about how you convinced Daddy to get on that sled and then gave him the ride of his life!"

"Mom, do you remember that time we were on a camping vacation in Maine on our way to Prince Edward Island, and the bugs were so horrible when we were trying to eat supper? Remember Judy and me, sitting on the same side of the picnic table with you and Daddy, and the picnic table standing straight up in the air, throwing all of us on the ground? There was so much screaming and laughing that the entire campground stopped and looked at us."

Oh, my friend, this is just the beginning of the treasure trove of stories in my family. Remind me someday to tell you about the time we were in a camping trailer, and it rolled into the lake. Shades of Lucy, Ricky, Fred, and Ethel and kids, if they had kids.

Mom was gifted in many other ways too. She was a talented and beloved music teacher in the school system and frequently gave private piano lessons. At the time of this story, my parents were missionaries in Concord, New Hampshire. Somehow Mom was asked to go to the New Hampshire State Mental Hospital once a month to play the piano for the women housed there. She thought, "What a kind and good thing to do," and off she went one cold winter night. When she returned home, she was a different woman, with quite a few stories to tell.

For the record, I can honestly say that she never stopped talking about the experiences she encountered that night and the other nights she played for the women there.

The Lesson in Hurry, Hurry, Hurry

When Mom arrived at the hospital, the nurse in charge ushered her through wards and wards of women. Each ward had a door that the nurse unlocked and locked it behind them. Mom felt quite unsettled as they went deeper and deeper into the caverns of the facility, locked in with unstable women

"It was scary!" she told me. "I thought I would never get out."

Finally they arrived at the women's ward where Mom was to play the piano. The women were wandering around, and several wanted to meet her and talk to her immediately. One of them marched right up to Mom and said, "Please don't think I am crazy. I have had two sets of twins, back to back, and I just cannot handle it anymore."

Mom quickly replied, "Honey, if I had had two sets of twins, back to back, I would be right in here with you!"

The nurse led Mom to the piano. Quite a few women milled around as she took her seat, very curious about her, waiting for her to start playing.

Soon a nurse brought a woman to the piano and somehow—I don't know how—made the woman sit on the floor. The nurse tied her to the leg of the piano and promptly went on break. Yes, the nurse tied her . . . and then left Mom all alone! So here is Mom, no guards or nurses around, starting to play several songs with her eyes riveted on the lady who is tied to the piano and inching her way closer and closer to Mom.

Knowing my mom, I would say that most likely her first big, rousing song to play was "Roll Out the Barrel." It's a great icebreaker! That song was always the first on the list of her repertoire, and she could never sit still when she played it! She would bounce up the bench and then down the bench, up the bench and then back down the bench—pounding that spirited tune and singing too. I think that both that piano and the bench took a beating that night. As I said, she was quite talented: she could play "Roll Out the Barrel" on the accordion too. Trust me, I heard it all my life.

But remember, this time Mom was keeping her eyes peeled on the mentally disturbed and bound lady who, from time to time, would look up at her from the floor and holler, "Why don't you play 'The Star-Spangled Banner'?"

Mom told me, "Becky, I played several songs and then finally, at my new friend's urging, ripped right into 'The Star-Spangled Banner.' The women stood up, placed their hands over their hearts, and sang with spirit and patriotism! When I finished, they all sat down, and the tied lady looked up at me and said, 'That was nice—what was that?'"

On one of these occasions, a nurse made this comment to Mom, "Mrs. Fowler, most people who are in this hospital are here because of guilt." Interesting perception, don't you think? Guilt. Something happened to them that they could not handle or caused them to blame themselves for everything—to the point that they had to be institutionalized.

Mom always commiserated with one particular woman. She is the sad part of this story. She just sat in a chair, her body rocking back and forth, saying repeatedly, "Hurry. Hurry. Hurry." Mom always said that when she saw this woman, she thought to herself, "There I am. That's me."

Why, you ask? Because Mom was always in a hurry. She was like Edith Bunker—she ran everywhere. She couldn't walk across the room, she had to leap across the room. None of her family could move fast enough for her. When other babies' first words were, "Da-da and Ma-ma," I am certain Mom's were "Faster, faster, faster!" She lived like she drove a car—seventy miles an hour, frequently telling me, "We've got to get there!" There were classes to be taught, people to meet, food to be fixed, the gospel to be shared, problems to be solved, a soul to be encouraged, and a million other things that busy Christian women know all about. There never was enough time. And sometimes Mom collapsed.

My sister, is this rocking woman you too? Do you identify with her?

Hurry, hurry, hurry—running too hard, running too fast, and completely exhausted.

Hurry, hurry, hurry to the point that you have completely lost yourself. You've come a long way, baby, living your life on the edge and trying to keep up with the world's suffocating stress.

Running, running, running . . . and feeling like you are getting nowhere. Just like a hamster on its crazy, spinning wheel. Hurry, hurry, hurry until finally there is a nervous breakdown, a meltdown, a halt in production. Then you are no good to anybody. And all you can barely utter is, "Stop the world. I want to get off!"

What is the answer? God. It is always God. Our merciful Father looks down upon all His children and kindly says, "Be still and know that I am God" (Psalm 46:10 KJV).

MOMENTS IN PRAYER

Help me, O Lord. Help me to stop and be still. Help me to see You and Your time and what is important to You. Help me to focus on others and not on myself so much. Help me not to rush things but to enjoy just this day—this moment You so graciously have given me.

Help me to stop . . . and look . . . and listen to You.
Help me to take the time and seek the time for You.
O Lord, please help me to find time for You again.

*Young
Becky and Jeff*

I Am Woman, Hear Me Gasp!

Is this you? You feel like you are always in the car, driving as fast as you can to get the errands done, and the kids are clinging to the seats for dear life. You are always on the phone—speaking and texting—and simply do not have the time to answer anybody's questions. You feel like you are giving ninety-five percent to your job and only five percent to your family. You have a deadline; a child has a fever; your boss has called and wants you to call him back (it doesn't sound good); there is absolutely no food in the house; and the dog has just thrown up on your favorite bedspread.

Sound familiar? Welcome to the world of the American woman. Now, there may be a few variations, but in general, this is your life. You have arrived; society tells you "you've come a long way, baby!" You can sing right along with the woman on the television commercial, dressed in a power suit, stilettos, and brandishing a skillet: "I can bring home the bacon, fry it up in a pan, and never let you forget you're a man. 'Cause I'm a woman; W-O-M-A-N!"

Are you running too hard, my sister? Do you barely have enough time to eat and help the kids with their homework? Are you always multitasking in the car and texting furiously? Is your plate full and overflowing with details, ideas, and deadlines? How many times have you seriously thought about donating your firstborn to someone just so you could have a nap? And the hope of just five minutes to yourself is just that—hope.

In the 1980s, *Time* magazine did a survey on the American woman—the Superwoman. And at the end of the survey was this statement: "The American woman has earned one right—the right to be exhausted!" That was over thirty years ago!

I saw this anonymous quote on Pinterest:

> It's hard to be a woman.
> You must think like a man,
> Act like a lady,
> Look like a young girl,
> And work like a horse!

I think I hear someone in the background saying, "Amen, preach it, sister! Ain't that the truth!"

I remember discussing this Superwoman topic with my mom, quoting a then-popular song line, "I am woman, hear me roar!" My mom quickly retorted, "It ought to be, 'I am woman, hear me gasp!'" Or maybe this is better, "I am woman, hear me scream" because when you are stressed, running, working, and trying to manage a household, you find yourself wanting to scream.

We all have heard, "Laugh and the world laughs with you. Cry and you cry alone." Somewhere I read, "Laugh and the world laughs with you. Cry and you cry with your girlfriends!" So true. How important women are to women! We females absolutely, unequivocally need one another, and friendships are a necessity in our lives. Men do not necessarily cultivate friendships after they are married, as they turn to their wives for most things. But it has been my take that women always surround themselves with girlfriends to do lunch, talk, text, and email. That is a given—probably because God made us this way. Girl babies begin talking sooner than boy babies—that is proven scientifically.

God is so smart. He knows the importance of communication in a family. Ninety-nine percent of the time, who starts the discussions?

It is Mama. Who talks to the kids and the husband and has a pretty good idea about the happenings of her home? It is Mama. We are verbal and vocal—we want to be heard, and we definitely want to express our opinions. We do know how to roar, don't we?

> Did you ever stop to consider why God made women more verbal than men? He knew who would be spending the most time with the children. Women are quick and skillful at nurturing, caring, teaching, and honing in on what is important for their children. We are naturals at seeing needs and identifying broken hearts and hurting homes. We are spiritual creatures that are sensitive to God and to His will for our families.[1]

Remember Tammy Wynette's song, "Stand by Your Man"? It begins, "Sometimes it's hard to be a woman." Yes, it is hard to be a woman. It never has been easy. Life is downright difficult! Just ask Eve. I think we all want relief, deliverance, and answers. And only God can help us. God knows our hearts; He has all the answers and will supply all our needs. God can do anything! I think we ought to get down on our knees every day and thank God for God, and that He is in charge!

Too often we expect God to drop everything and run to us, fixing our problems continually. We know He is "on call" 24/7; God never sleeps. "He will not allow your foot to slip; He who keeps you will not slumber. Behold, He who keeps Israel will neither slumber nor sleep" (Psalm 121:3–4).

We frequently quote to ourselves and others: "I [God] will never leave you nor forsake you" (Hebrews 13:5 KJV). God is always near, right? Right. What a comforting passage; we should quote it a lot.

What Can God Expect from Us?

Have we ever thought about what God expects? Do we find the time for Him? Do we talk to Him in prayer and read His mighty, life-altering word daily? Are we as committed to Him as He is to us? Do we reciprocate by being ready to do His will 24/7?

How do we practice those beautiful words spoken through David when he wrote in Psalm 46:10, "Be still and know that I am God"? How do we accomplish that? Who has time to be still in the first place?

How does the woman of God seek precious moments with Him? Hear the answer: She learns to stop everything and takes the time. She makes time for the Master who knows all, loves all, controls all, heals all, and saves all. She arranges her day so that she is able to be Mary and sit at Jesus' feet. She prays throughout the day like Daniel did. She even finds quiet times early or late in the day to talk to the Father like Jesus did.

This is a learned process. I speak only from my experience. I always knew that I loved God and wanted to please Him in all things. But I had to grow, study the Bible, suffer, be delivered, and rejoice in His magnificent love to see the importance of spending time with Him.

Pause and Ponder

How are you challenged to seek the precious moments for God daily? Why? Share.

The Work in You

I have read Philippians 1:6 at least a hundred times, but today it finally hit home with me. Paul, inspired by the Holy Spirit, wrote: "For I am confident of this very thing, that He who began a good work in you will perfect it until the day of Christ Jesus."

Who is the one who began the good work in the Philippian Christians? It is God, of course. This marvelous church of sacrificial-giving brethren began on a riverbank with the conversion of a businesswoman named Lydia. By the time Paul writes to them from a prison in Rome, approximately eleven years later, the church has grown into a strong congregation that includes elders and deacons (Acts 16:11–40; Philippians 1:1).

What a dynamic, loving, and generous church. We can certainly call the church at Philippi "the church with the *big* heart!" It is understandable that this church is so dear to Paul's heart. From the Scriptures we learn that this congregation supported Paul and frequently sent messengers with gifts for him. As Paul expressed his love for them frequently in the book of Philippians, we can certainly feel their mutual love for him.

> Nevertheless, you have done well to share with me in my affliction. You yourselves also know, Philippians, that at the first preaching of the gospel, after I left Macedonia, no church shared with me in the matter of giving and receiving but you alone; or even in Thessalonica you sent a gift more than once for my needs (Philippians 4:14–16).

You see, when they became Christians, God's work began in their lives. And what did the Philippians do? They grew the church. They served. They sacrificed, and they spread the good news, the gospel of Jesus Christ. They loved and gave their all. They knew how to rejoice, and they knew great sorrow. They surrendered all and went to work. They found time for God.

God's work has begun in our lives also, my sisters, and what work are we doing for Him in return? Will we, like Paul, call ourselves a bond-servant of Christ Jesus—one who never wants to be free? Will we willingly offer ourselves as a living sacrifice for God (Romans 12:1)? Will we find the time to serve Him and give our money to help support missionaries across this earth? Will we ourselves go and be that missionary? Will we be daily Bible readers and good Bible students who pray every day? Will we be faithful and love our church family? Will we be bold for Jesus and help the lost find their way home to Him? Will we repeat Jesus' words, "We must work the works of Him who sent Me as long as it is day; night is coming when no one can work" (John 9:4)?

Or are we so busy trying to earn a living and raise the young 'uns that we have forgotten about God? Or could it possibly be that we simply do not want to invest the time and energy it takes to have a relationship with God and think on spiritual things? Do we serve God only on Sunday and serve Satan Monday through Saturday? Is it hard for us to get up and go to the Lord's house on Sunday after partying all Saturday night?

Let's be honest with ourselves—we know our lifestyles. Mother often said: "We women certainly find the time for everything we want to do!" We find the money to purchase those things we've been drooling over. Even when the money is tight and the budget is thin, we figure out a way to obtain what our heart desires. We've heard the old saying, "Where there is a will, there is a way." Is it true? Do we find the time for what we want to do?

Godly Women

How do Christian men value women who take time to know God?

> My Grandma Reynolds showed me the way of the Lord; my mother taught me the gospel of Christ; my wife is escorting me to heaven; my daughter holds fast to the teachings of Jesus; and my sister-in-law loves the Lord's church. How fortunate I am. What did I do to deserve to be around such godly women? I made the choice to surround myself with them.
>
> Boaz married Ruth because he had learned of her loyalty and willingness to serve the God of Israel. He also knew the character of her mother-in-law Naomi and chose to surround himself with godly women. What did that do for him? It redeemed him and led him into the lineage of Christ.
>
> What did Queen Esther do when confronted with the extinction of her people? She walked in the way of the Lord. She didn't wring her hands, hide, or run from danger. She stood up for what was right and trusted in the God of Israel. Rahab believed, understood, took action, and was responsible for saving her whole family. Our Lord needs godly women to teach the gospel and work in His ways to save mankind. Surround yourself with godly women; they will make a difference in your life.[2]

Pause and Ponder

Write your thoughts about being a woman as described above. What qualities must you develop?

Stop, my sister. Stop and think and consider: Being a Christian woman is your highest calling. It is the greatest honor you will ever know in this life. Being God's daughter is the most supreme honor and blessing a woman can realize, and surrendering to Him is the key. But Satan works overtime to turn your head in his direction. Satan wants you depressed, negative, exhausted, and insecure. But God wants you to be happy, positive, energized, and secure. Which do you really want?

The Sin of Neglect

I love to look at the parables of Jesus, don't you? His style of teaching was dynamic and to the point. Jesus did not have time to "pretty up" a story or please a certain group of people. He was the Son of Man on a mission as the Son of God. He was the Master Teacher—the Ultimate Rabbi—with much to say, and His time on earth was fleeting.

From the poorest to the richest, from the humblest to the proudest, the multitudes that followed Jesus surely went home with profound spiritual teachings from Jesus' parables. He taught with a powerhouse punch, and don't you imagine there were many lively discussions among the people as they walked back to their villages? Wouldn't you have loved to have been in on those discussions?

Read the parable of the talents from Matthew 25:14–30. You know the story, but it helps to read it again. The master, preparing for a journey, gave three of his servants money—talents. To one he gave five talents, to another he gave two talents, and to the last he gave one talent. Each was given "according to his own ability," so we know that all three had at least one talent—a play on words.

The first two servants doubled their talents while the third servant simply protected his. He even told his master that he was scared and dug a hole and hid the money.

What was the reaction of the master? "You wicked, lazy slave." Wicked for blaming the master instead of himself and lazy because he didn't want to be bothered with taking care of his master's possessions. He even refused to take the talent to the bank and gain interest. The easiest thing was to do nothing. And that is exactly what he did—nothing. That servant was called "worthless" and thrown into outer darkness where there is much wailing and gnashing of teeth. That scene is one of great misery—hell.

This word "lazy" always startles me. The third servant did not wish to take the time to do something for his master who had given him the talent and ability to use it. He did not even have enough energy to fear what his master could do to him. Lazy, lazy, lazy. May that word never describe you and me, my sister. That lazy servant never thought to seek precious moments for his master, and he paid for it in eternal torment.

> When he (Christ) comes, the slothful and unprofitable will be cast out not because they did not believe, or because they had rebelled, but because they had neglected the opportunities which he had committed to them.[3]

Desires of Your Heart Include God

May I give you a life-changing scripture, my sister? "Delight yourself in the Lord; and He will give you the desires of your heart" (Psalm 37:4).

Delight yourself—not somebody else, but yourself. Discover God; find the joy in the Father and His Word; immerse yourself in pleasing Him; love, work, and live every moment in this life for Jehovah; let your world revolve around your Father. What will be the result? God will give you everything you want and need. He will open the windows of heaven and absolutely amaze you by pouring blessings on top of blessings on your head. As you ponder this passage, please remember two things:

(1) God knows how to give and when to give, and (2) delighting yourself in God takes time, labor, and a servant's heart.

A life lived for God is the only life worth living. And as we serve, love, worship, and obey the Lord, we find the one thing we have been searching for all along: happiness—all wrapped up in the garb of peace. Happiness occurs when we give ourselves away to God. And *give* is the defining word here. There are two types of people in this world: givers and takers. Which one describes you?

Don't Forget God

Too often on this harried journey we call life, we humans can easily make the biggest mistake of our lives: we forget God! It has happened before. God is not shocked at our behavior. His own children forgot Him in the Old Testament. Let's see what God had to say about this.

> My people are destroyed for lack of knowledge. Because you have rejected knowledge, I also will reject you from being My priest. Since you have forgotten the law of your God, I also will forget your children (Hosea 4:6).

> It shall come about if you ever forget the Lord your God and go after other gods and serve them and worship them, I testify against you today that you will surely perish (Deuteronomy 8:19).

> A voice is heard on the bare heights, the weeping and the supplications of the sons of Israel; because they have perverted their way, they have forgotten the Lord their God (Jeremiah 3:21).

Pause and Ponder

Read each of the above verses aloud. Underline the consequences of forgetting God.

I see warnings, peril, and sadness in store when we forget to "delight ourselves in the Lord." We can never say that God is not explicit when it comes to His promises of punishment for those who forget Him and serve other gods. He will do what He says—He always has.

We forget God too. It's our human nature. We need constant reminding of our Father's presence, His love, His goodness, and His power. We neglect to recall His overwhelming passion for His children and His constant desire for a relationship with us. Read the Old Testament and see how many times God delivered His children, especially when they had forsaken Him. Keith Parker once said, "God is crazy about you!" How often do we forget that?

Satan loves it when we have spiritual Alzheimer's disease. It makes us forget that God is our Father. We forget that He can make our lives better. We forget the power of prayer. We forget that He has all the answers. We forget that He has a marvelous plan for our lives (Jeremiah 29:11). We forget that Jesus' blood can wash every sin away. And sadly, we forget to stop and gaze at that cross on Calvary and the empty tomb that changed everything! I positively believe that God's foresight in the Lord's supper being observed weekly is because we humans too quickly forget the body and blood that were given so freely on Calvary.

It is easy to become the wicked and lazy servant who couldn't be bothered with his master's business. As hard as it is to believe, many Christians do not want to seek precious moments to read the Master's Word, the Bible, or to pray to Him daily. Having a relationship with Jesus is not on their list of priorities.

And so, right now I ask you two important questions, my sister, "What is the work that God has begun in you?" and "Are you finding the time to do it?"

> This is the beginning of a new day.
> God has given me this day to use as I will.
> I can waste it or use it for good,
> But what I do today is important
> Because I am exchanging a day of my life for it.
> When tomorrow comes, this day will be gone forever,

Leaving in its place something I have traded for it.
I want it to be a gain and not a loss; good and not evil;
Success and not failure, in order that I shall not
Regret the price I paid for it today.

—Author unknown[4]

MOMENTS IN PRAYER

Oh Lord, please help me seek precious moments for You with every breath. Please help me to keep my priorities straight and keep You at the top of every possible list. I love You with all my heart, and pleasing You is all I want to do. In Jesus' name, Amen.

Moments in Song

"All of Self and None of Thee" and "Anywhere with Jesus"

KEEP SEEKING

1. Read Philippians 1:6 out loud. Write it. Memorize it.
2. What is the work that God has begun in you?
3. How are you doing that work for Him?
4. How are you using your talents?
5. What is the first thing you can start doing today to use one of your talents?

Timely Quotes

"We all have possibilities we don't know about. We can do things we don't even dream we can do."

—Dale Carnegie

"If it's important to you, you'll find a way.
If it's not, you'll find an excuse!"

—Ryan Blair

"For every minute that you are angry you
lose sixty seconds of happiness."

—Ralph Waldo Emerson

Two Strangers

It was a Delta flight from Atlanta to Indianapolis. My dad had passed away two weeks previously, and my heart was very heavy. If you have experienced the sudden death of a loved one, the shock, the funeral, the burial, then you know what I am talking about.

One of the very first emotions I felt was that I would never smile again. How could I ever be happy again? Like zombies, our family staggered through the motions. Then we went back to our respective homes after the funeral. And it was time for me to fly to a speaking engagement.

I boarded the airplane and took a seat next to a nice gentleman. "David" and I chatted a bit, getting acquainted. He was headed home after business dealings in Atlanta, my home. Conversation was easy. We were about the same age, he was courteous, and like me, he was married with children.

Somewhere in the middle of that Delta flight, I told David that my dad had just passed away and he was my first parent to lose. I described some of the details, but I didn't have to describe my deep sorrow. David told me that he had lost his dad the year before. His story was not like mine in that his dad had suffered for about a year before his death. In sharp contrast, my dad had simply gotten out of bed, dressed, gone outside to sharpen the blade on the lawnmower, came back into his bedroom, and dropped dead.

As David talked about his relationship with his dad and his love for him, he started to tear up. I reached over and patted his hand and nodded. I knew what he was feeling. He continued to tell me about how much he missed his father.

I just kept nodding my head. We spent the rest of the flight talking about our parents and how much we loved them.

As the plane landed, David told me that he had been planning to go to his office that morning, but now he wasn't so sure. He wanted to be with his family instead. I remember saying, "Go home. That's where you need to be."

We taxied to the gate, gathered our things, and deplaned. We walked up the jet bridge together, entered the concourse, and gave each other a goodbye hug. We were like old friends, comrades in sorrow—two "Baby Boomers" trying to keep on living.

Now I know that is a very odd story. It is odd to me—even to this day. But I believe that God sends people into our lives to help us, and He also sends people for us to help. And sometimes it happens on an airplane. I believe that God sent this businessman to me because I needed to know someone's perspective on a father's death. It was important for me to hear someone else's feelings on the matter. I hope I helped David in some way.

We are going to have unusual and different encounters in our lifetime. We won't be able to ascertain immediately what they are about—we may never know. God will give us the time to ponder about these events. I believe God sent comfort through each of us. All I can tell you is that David helped me to smile again.

The First Time

Tap, tap, tap.
What was that?
Rap, rap, rap.
There it goes again. What is that?
Knock, knock, knock.
And a voice calls through the door:
"It's Me, child. It's Jesus. Open the door and let Me in. It is time."

Behold, I stand at the door and knock; if anyone hears My voice and opens the door, I will come in to him and will dine with him, and he with Me (Revelation 3:20).

You may have not recognized this scene in your life, but most likely it has occurred. Think about it. Think about the times when Jesus has called you. How many invitation songs knocked on the door of your heart before you finally responded? Did a preacher step on your toes and urge you to change your life? Maybe you were invited to a gospel meeting, or were wondering about what a certain scripture meant, or perhaps you have even been studying your Bible lesson for Sunday and more questions popped into your head. What did you do, my friend? Did you answer Jesus' call? Did you go to that gospel meeting? Did you dig deeper into the word of God? Did you take the time to ask, seek, and knock? Did you have the desire to learn and grow?

Relationship Builders: Let Him In; Keep His Word

Jesus stood at the door of your heart, calling with more opportunities for you to learn and more blessings for you to receive. What did you do? Perhaps you did nothing. Maybe you were simply too busy for Him. You had other things on your mind that were more important. Or maybe you responded. Perhaps you opened the door and let Jesus in.

According to Revelation 4:11, mankind was created by God's will or pleasure. Doesn't it stand to reason that the Father wants to hear from His children? Why wouldn't the Creator want a relationship with the created?

When we open the door of our hearts to Him, the relationship begins. God does not want us to grab a fast bite at the drive-thru somewhere, throw the sack out the window, and just keep flying down the crazy road we live on. But He is willing to spend precious moments with us, communicating back and forth through our prayers and His word given us by the Spirit.

My friends, we are invited to the feast of a lifetime, and this feast will continue into eternity. It is not going to be a minute here or a minute there, but there will be hours of precious time like no other we have ever known. However, Jesus never forces His way into our lives. It is up to us to open the door. Do we want that?

Jesus once said, "If anyone loves Me, he will keep My word; and My Father will love him, and We will come to him and make Our abode with him" (John 14:23). Living together is the result of love—our love and their love.

When Jesus lives with us, we let Him come in and rearrange the furniture. We submit to Him and treasure His words. It is joy to listen to Him, knowing that He instructs us for our own good.

> Where sincere love to Christ is in the heart, there will be obedience. Love will be a commanding, constraining principle; and where love is, duty follows from a principle of gratitude. God will not only love obedient believers, but he will take pleasure in loving them, will rest

in love to them. He will be with them as his home. These privileges are confined to those whose faith worketh by love, and whose love to Jesus leads them to keep his commandments.[5]

Have we thought about the fact that God and Jesus live with us, but we have to do our part?

We must first love Jesus and keep His word. We can dine with Him and live with Him. What more could anyone want? And yet people still reject Jesus. When Jesus was born, there was no room at the inn in Bethlehem, and people today still do not have room for Him.

Sister, pull up a chair and sit by me. Let's draw near to God and hear what He has to say. Let's take the time to find out more about our Father. Will you join me as we open the door and let Him in?

Pause and Ponder

Write John 14:23, substituting your name for each lowercase pronoun.

Time Begins

God begins His message with these words: "In the beginning." *Genesis* simply means "the beginning." Two particular scriptures—one from the Old Testament and one from the New Testament—speak about "the beginning" when God's story began.

- In the beginning God created the heavens and the earth (Genesis 1:1).
- In the beginning was the Word, and the Word was with God, and the Word was God (John 1:1).

God, Jesus, and the Holy Spirit created the world. They all were present at creation. The word for *God* in Genesis 1 is *Elohim,* and it is plural, meaning all three beings of the godhead were present. In the New Testament, the *Word* that was with God was Jesus, the Son of God.

In the beginning God [Elohim] created the heavens and the earth. The earth was formless and void, and darkness was over the surface of the deep, and the Spirit of God was moving over the surface of the waters (Genesis 1:1–2).

The first day and night were created on the first day of Creation—the first twenty-four-hour day. God created time! There were five more days of creation, and then the last, a day of rest. At the end of each day, "God saw that it was good." But I particularly like that on the sixth day when God created man and woman, He said it was "very good."

The word *time* is used some 626 times in the New American Standard Bible and is defined as "the indefinite continued progress of existence and events in the past, present, and future regarded as a whole."

It's not easy to define or describe time. How would you define it? Time is all around us and continually in our minds as we organize the days, minutes, and seconds of life. Time is essential, and we cannot live without it. Time categorizes our lives into days, months, and years, as well as lifetimes, eras, eons, and millenniums.

A missionary went to Africa to live and teach the word of God. He was a very busy man and could readily be seen talking to people, meeting people in the village, and teaching classes. He was completely unaware of the countless times he glanced at his watch and then hurried off to do something else. Finally an African stopped him and asked, "Who is the god on your arm?" It certainly is possible to let time dictate our every move. Are we slaves to a schedule?

Number of Days

In his wonderful Psalm 139, David describes the omniscience, the omnipresence, and the omnipotence of God—the three O's. Take the time to read each marvelous verse, but for right now, let us focus on the number of days we will live physically:

Your eyes have seen my unformed substance; and in Your book were all written the days that were ordained for me, when as yet there was not one of them (Psalm 139:16).

What amazing and beautiful thoughts! W. E. Addis remarked about this verse: "This passage declares that the psalmist's days were preordained by God and visible to Him long before they had actual existence."[6]

God knew you and me even before we were conceived. He had already decided how many days we would live even before we took our first breath. It makes sense that our mighty God would know everything about our time on earth because He created it.

Have You Ever Wondered?

Why are you here right now? Have you questioned why you were born to your parents and raised in a particular town and state?

I asked my husband these questions one night as he was sitting up in bed.

"Jeff, have you ever wondered why you were born to the parents you have and why you were raised in the city you lived during that time?"

He looked at me very calmly and replied, "Nope." And then he rolled over and went to sleep. I think he was avoiding me.

Well, Jeff may not have ever wondered about these things, but I have! Why did the Father place me in this time period? Movies fantasize and romanticize the days of Jane Austen, Scarlett O'Hara, and Anne of Green Gables. But the reality is that God is the one who placed us where we are, in this time period, born to our parents. Why? God has a work for us to do.

God may send us across the seas to a foreign mission field, or He may place us in a mission field here in America, or perhaps we may live in the same town all our lives. But those years of growing up here, there, and yon have shaped us into the Christian women we are today. Even in times past when life was difficult and we questioned many situations, God was working things out for our good so that we could do

His good: "And we know that God causes all things to work together for good to those who love God, to those who are called according to His purpose" (Romans 8:28).

Pause and Ponder

Read Psalm 16:6 and discuss.

For Such a Time

The old saying, "Bloom where you are planted," packs a powerful punch for most Christians, because we want to please our Father with fruitful and meaningful lives in His service. Often we wonder, "Are we accomplishing anything in this community?" Mordecai's words to Esther definitely ring in our ears and hearts, "Who knows whether you have not attained royalty for such a time as this?" (Esther 4:14). No, we are not Persian queens, but we are daughters of the King, and He has planted us where we are "for such a time as this." God has a purpose and a work for us to do.

Our God made time and man, and He gave man the stewardship of his days here on this earth. You and I have the freedom to decide how, why, and where we will spend each moment, each hour, and each day.

Early Times

As we read the Bible, we see how God first revealed the passage of time.

> Now the man had relations with his wife Eve, and she conceived and gave birth to Cain, and she said, "I have gotten a manchild with the help of the Lord." Again, she gave birth to his brother Abel. And Abel was a keeper of flocks, but Cain was a tiller of the ground. So it came about in the course of time that Cain brought an offering to the Lord of the fruit of the ground (Genesis 4:1–3).

It is interesting to note that it is possible that Cain and Abel were twins because Eve gives birth twice, but the Scriptures use the word *conceived* only once. (Something to consider.)

Then the text says, "It came about in the course of time." How much time? We don't know. However, some years had passed—enough at least to know that Cain and Abel were not the only children of Adam and Eve. Also this first family was accustomed to offering sacrifices to the Lord.

When we read this famous account of the first murder, we see that eventually Cain is exiled to a place where he is afraid whoever finds him will kill him. Who would hurt Cain? It had to be his relatives. And time certainly had to pass for there to be a different place from where Cain originally lived, another city with people related to him.

> Cain said to the Lord, "My punishment is too great to bear! Behold, You have driven me this day from the face of the ground; and from Your face I will be hidden, and I will be a vagrant and a wanderer on the earth, and whoever finds me will kill me" (Genesis 4:13–14).

Adam died at the very old age of 930 (Genesis 5:5). The current rule of thumb today is that a generation consists of approximately twenty-five years. If we divide those twenty-five years into 930, we will obtain 37.2. Hard as it is to comprehend, God let Adam live 930 years, and Adam was the father of approximately 37 generations of people.

A Miracle of Time

King Hezekiah was very ill, but the Lord decided to give him fifteen more years to live. Hezekiah asked for a sign that this was so. He even asked God to turn the sundial back ten steps. God granted the king's request, and time went backward. Quite a miracle! As we know, that was impossible. But with God, nothing is impossible.

> "Shall the shadow go forward ten steps or go back ten steps?" So Hezekiah answered, "It is easy for the shadow to decline ten steps; no, but let the shadow turn backward ten steps." Isaiah the prophet

cried to the Lord, and He brought the shadow on the stairway back ten steps (2 Kings 20:8).

God Rules Time

Look what God did in the middle of a battle for Joshua.

> Then Joshua spoke to the Lord in the day when the Lord delivered up the Amorites before the sons of Israel, and he said in the sight of Israel, "O sun, stand still at Gibeon, and O moon in the valley of Aijalon." So the sun stood still, and the moon stopped, until the nation avenged themselves of their enemies. Is it not written in the book of Jashar? And the sun stopped in the middle of the sky and did not hasten to go down for about a whole day. There was no day like that before it or after it, when the Lord listened to the voice of a man; for the Lord fought for Israel (Joshua 10:12–14).

The sun stopped in its orbit. Now girls, only God could do that!

Notice also what Daniel had to say about the power of God and time: "Let the name of God be blessed forever and ever, for wisdom and power belong to Him. It is He who changes the times and the epochs; He removes kings and establishes kings" (Daniel 2:20–21).

It is our God who has the power to change times and epochs. What is an epoch? It is an era, an age, a period of time. Only God can stop and start time and periods of time as He pleases, because He is the Father of time!

Not Eastern, Central, Mountain, or Pacific

God's time is not our time! How extremely difficult for any twenty-first century American to grasp that fact; we are accustomed to express lanes and fast checkouts. We are a spoiled society; we want our answers now, and it's all about us. That's the American way. Faster, faster, faster!

God says, "No. You humans are on My time, not your time. Child of mine, be patient. I am in charge and all is well. Slow down and wait for Me. I know what is best for you and when."

We pray and desire an answer right now—or even yesterday! Sometimes He does answer immediately, but sometimes He does not. God has an answering system: *yes, no,* and *not right now.* We must learn to wait on God.

He teaches us this waiting principle by having inspired Isaiah and David to write these words:

> Yet those who wait for the Lord will gain new strength; they will mount up with wings like eagles, they will run and not get tired, they will walk and not become weary (Isaiah 40:31).

> My soul waits in silence for God only; from Him is my salvation . . . My soul, wait in silence for God only, for my hope is from Him (Psalm 62:1, 5).

Pause and Ponder

Read all twelve verses of Psalm 62. Give Bible definitions of the words *wait, hope,* and *rock.* Why is the word *silence* important?

Be Still

We must learn to be still and wait on the Father. It is a lesson of patience for us, His creation. We must learn to let God work, and that is a hard lesson for us. In the process we will realize that His time is absolutely right, perfect, and just. Waiting on God is a faith builder, and wisdom teaches us to have patience and learn the lesson God is trying to teach us. Choosing to live for God enables us to have the most blessed life ever, no matter what God decides. Waiting on God teaches us to trust Him more.

Life itself—the ebb and flow of it—is a gift from God. He is there, helping us understand the nitty-gritty daily grind, the joys, the euphorias, and the dark sorrows too. Whatever the disaster—the crisis, the emergency, the problem that has us begging on our knees—it will be resolved. We must have more faith in God. Even when I read Jesus' words in Matthew 6:11, "Give us this day our daily bread," I see comfort and reassurance. Jesus tells us not to worry about our "future" bread—just be concerned about today's.

Answers and peace will flow from our God in His time because we belong to Him, and the Master Designer always has a plan. God can fix anything and perform beyond what we are able to imagine. We need to increase our trust and faith. I love what Jeremiah and Paul had to say about God.

> Ah Lord God! Behold, You have made the heavens and the earth by Your great power and by Your outstretched arm! Nothing is too difficult for You (Jeremiah 32:17).

> Now to Him who is able to do far more abundantly beyond all that we ask or think, according to the power that works within us, to Him be the glory in the church and in Christ Jesus to all generations forever and ever. Amen (Ephesians 3:20–21).

Wise is the child of God who calmly steps back and lets God rule in every aspect of her life. Hopefully, our faith kicks in. From experience, we realize we cannot tell the Father what to do. We will not win in that department. But we must remember that we are loved; He knows our hearts, and He knows what is best. We must be at peace and be comforted with the powerful passage from Exodus 14:14: "The Lord will fight for you while you keep silent."

It's the keeping *silent* part that is hard for Ol' Beck. I want to mouth off and tell everyone my problems, my opinion—whatever. But then I remind myself that I have surrendered to my Father and that I am a child of the King. Whatever it is, I have to leave it at my Father's feet and walk away. And that brings peace, for I have learned God's way is the best way. That takes time to learn.

Therein lies your life and my life. God's will, will be done. Every single time. "We walk by faith, not by sight" (2 Corinthians 5:7).

O, may I learn, in every state,
To make His will my own,
And when the joys of sense depart,
To walk with Him alone.

—Unknown

MOMENTS IN PRAYER

Oh, Lord, I pray today for peace in my life and in the world. I thank You for protecting me and my family and for fighting our battles daily. Lord, Your will be done on earth as it is in heaven. I am the sheep of Your hand and Your pasture. I look to You for everything in this life and in the life to come. Please don't give up on me, and please don't stop loving me. In Jesus' name I pray, Amen.

Moments in Song

"Who at the Door Is Standing?" and "Let the Savior In"

KEEP SEEKING

1. When Jesus knocks on the door of our hearts, what should we do?
2. What does it mean for you to "wait on the Lord"?

Timely Quotes

"Yesterday's the past, tomorrow's the future, but today
is a gift. That's why it's called the present."

—Bill Keane

"Know the true value of time; snatch, seize, and enjoy every moment of it. No idleness, no laziness, no procrastination: never put off till tomorrow what you can do today."
—Philip Stanhope, 4th Earl of Chesterfield

"You can't be brave if you've only had wonderful things happen to you."
—Mary Tyler Moore

There Is a Time For Everything

There is an appointed time for everything.
And there is a time
For every event under heaven—
A time to give birth and a time to die;
A time to plant and a time to uproot what is planted.
A time to kill and a time to heal;
A time to weep and a time to laugh;
A time to mourn and a time to dance.
A time to throw stones and a time to gather stones;
A time to embrace and a time to shun embracing.
A time to search and a time to give up as lost;
A time to keep and a time to throw away.
A time to tear apart and a time to sew together;
A time to be silent and a time to speak.
A time to love and a time to hate;
A time for war and a time for peace.

—Ecclesiastes 3:1–8

*Jeff and
Becky Blackmon*

CHAPTER 3

"It's the Right Time!

Our Jehovah God knew before He created Adam and Eve and put them in that beautiful Paradise called Eden that they would sin there. God's plan for redemption was put into place long before man was ever created. God knew before creation that He would send His Son to die. Jesus coming to this earth and dying for a lost world was never plan B. "Just as He chose us in Him before the foundation of the world, that we would be holy and blameless before Him" (Ephesians 1:4).

> Inherent in this is the fact of God's calling and electing people before the foundation of the world; and very few theological questions have demanded more attention and interest than this. Clearly revealed in this is the fact that the coming of Jesus Christ into the world for the purpose of taking out of it a people for himself and redeeming them unto eternal life was no afterthought on God's part. Before the world was ever created, the divine plan of the Son of God's visitation of the human family existed in the eternal purpose of God. That body that Christ would gather from the populations of earth is destined to receive eternal life; because what God purposes is certain of fulfillment. Such a calling and election of those "in Christ" to receive eternal glory, however, is not capricious. Every man may decide if he will or will not become a part of it and receive the intended blessing.[7]

God's Perfect Timing

God did not send Jesus to this earth immediately following the sin in the Garden. No, He waited some four thousand years before that wonderful night in a Bethlehem stable when our Messiah was born to a precious young couple. Many years and events had to occur before Jesus, the perfect lamb of God, could be the perfect sacrifice—the perfect atonement—for all of us imperfect people. God had a mighty task on His hands—teaching His children to grow up.

Just think of all the people, places, and things that had to happen before Jesus arrived: The flood, the tower of Babel, Abraham, Isaac, Jacob, the twelve tribes, Egyptian bondage, three hundred years of idolatry, Moses, the old law, Joshua, the promised land, the judges, the kings, David, Solomon, the temple, the divided kingdom, Israel's constant immorality and idolatry, the major and minor prophets, the warnings from God, the Babylonian captivity, Daniel, Esther, God's deliverance of His children from Babylon, Ezra, and Nehemiah. And then add four hundred years of silence!

All these events were one momentous giant lesson God was teaching His people about His patience, His will, and His timing. All these things had to be put into place before Jesus could arrive, teach, die, be resurrected, and then return to God.

The Most Important Time

Consider the following verses explaining the fullness of time, including a time of redemption and adoption.

> But when the fullness of the time came, God sent forth His Son, born of a woman, born under the Law, so that He might redeem those who were under the Law, that we might receive the adoption as sons (Galatians 4:4–5).

Jesus came at just the right moment. God knew the exact second that Jesus would step foot on this earth. God also knew the exact moment when His Son would step foot into heaven again. Did it happen exactly as God had planned? Yes. Look at the first prophecy made in Eden when God told Satan: "I will put enmity between you and the woman, and between your seed and her seed; he shall bruise you on the head, and you shall bruise him on the heel" (Genesis 3:15).

Pause and Ponder

Discuss and explain the Genesis prophecy of Jesus' coming. Write out your Bible's translation of Galatians 4:4.

God sent Jesus to this earth at the perfect time: Roman roads were excellent; Greek language was well developed and widespread. Consider the following descriptions.

> The fullness of time . . . has the meaning of "at God's appointed time." All of the grand events of God's plan for the redemption of mankind were scheduled in advance, and from the beginning, even the final judgment itself being a planned and scheduled event.[8]

> The fulness of time is the perfect time in history, the time appointed by God the Father for His Son to be born, and later to die for the sins of the world. "Born of a woman" speaks of Christ's humanity and perhaps alludes to His role as the ultimate "Seed" of the woman. "Born under the Law" means Christ was subject to the Jewish law, further establishing His identification with all people who are subject to the Law. "Redeem," meaning to buy from the slave market, is a term used only by Paul in the New Testament. The verb describes Christ's supreme and final payment for the sins of humanity.[9]

> The apostle speaks of the "fulness of time," the precise time in history when the coming of Christ would be most ideal for the success of the Christian movement. This involves such things as the Old Testament Scriptures, the moral climate of the ancient world, geography, culture, language, transportation, political circumstances, etc. . . . The promise embraces both Jews and Gentiles.[10]

 Pause and Ponder

🌿 Copy Acts 15:18. What does that verse have to do with my adoption?

All of these thoughts about the fulness of time and God's salvation plans enable us to see the marvelous hand of God. His timing is mind boggling, don't you think? But so is His work in us. We are amazed at God's creation of our physical bodies. Likewise, we should be amazed at His design for our souls. Both go hand in hand.

It is crucial that we Christians read the Old Testament diligently and get a grasp of its content, geography, characters, and purpose. Then we can understand the constant and enduring love of God. Unfortunately, many Christians feel that the Old Testament is unnecessary. Nothing is further from the truth. The Old Testament is the New Testament concealed, and the New Testament is the Old Testament revealed.

The Wrong Time

It also is imperative that we read the New Testament relentlessly and look at the "times" Jesus mentioned. Note the time Jesus spent in His ministry. A young man of thirty (Luke 3:23), we know that He spent three years, teaching, performing miracles, and doing the will of His Father before it was time for Him to leave.

At the wedding feast in Cana, Jesus told His own mother, "Woman, what do I have to do with you? My hour has not yet come" (John 2:4). Jesus had not officially begun His ministry, but Jesus loved His mother and answered her request for help. This small glimpse into the relationship of Mary and Jesus shows their love for one another. Furthermore, I believe it shows Mary's faith in who He was—the Son of God. She knew He could remedy that wine problem at the wedding in Cana no matter what Jesus said to her. Don't you love this scene between mother and son? All we have recorded is Jesus telling her that His time has not come and the next verse where she instructs the servants at the wedding to do whatever Jesus says. I think Mary knew that this wedding needed help and fast! Jesus did what she asked Him to do—a miracle.

Pause and Ponder

Read John 7:6, 8, 30. What was this "time" Jesus was speaking about? Comment on Matthew 26:18. Discuss fulfillment of the Scriptures mentioned by Jesus in Luke 4:20–30.

Jesus' Full Schedule

I am amazed by the amount of work Jesus accomplished in his three-year ministry. He certainly made use of His time—every moment of every day. His level of energy was astounding. His typical twenty-four-hour day was maximized in teaching, healing, performing miracles, traveling from town to town, and especially preparing His apostles for their future work. Also, we must remember Jesus was constantly attacked by the prejudiced Pharisees who thought so highly of themselves. And don't forget the early morning hours and the evening times when He escaped to the desert or the Sea of Galilee or the Mount of Olives to pray. How easy it is to comprehend His collapsing into sleep on a boat in the middle of the lake unaware of a raging storm around Him.

Pause and Ponder

Compare your busy schedule with Jesus' schedule. How did He use precious moments to be with His Father? How do you plan to imitate Him more?

The Times of Ecclesiastes

Solomon describes life events beautifully in Ecclesiastes 3. Flip back a few pages to "Time with Becky" preceding this chapter. Haven't we all experienced most of these times in our own lives? Whether loving, laughing, embracing, shunning, tearing down, or mourning, we certainly have met moments like these face to face. One translation of Ecclesiastes 3:1 says, "There is a right time for everything." Yes, Ecclesiastes 3:1–8 is a very familiar passage. Song lyrics have even been written using the words.

Read these eight verses aloud and identify with them, remembering when these times happened to you personally or in the world around you. Evidently these times must have happened to Solomon too.

Moments Worth Noting

How often have we stopped and pondered the passage about "fighting the good fight" from 2 Timothy 4? It is stirring and inspiring to say the least, and a favorite too. Let's read 2 Timothy 4:1–8 and then take it apart.

- *At all times.* "I solemnly charge you in the presence of God and of Christ Jesus, who is to judge the living and the dead, and by His appearing and His kingdom: preach the word; be ready in season and out of season; reprove, rebuke, exhort, with great patience and instruction" (2 Timothy 4:1–2).

- *Another time coming.* "For the time will come when they will not endure sound doctrine; but wanting to have their ears tickled, they will accumulate for themselves teachers in accordance to their own desires, and will turn away their ears from the truth and will turn aside to myths" (2 Timothy 4:3–4).

- *Time to endure and work.* "But you, be sober in all things, endure hardship, do the work of an evangelist, fulfill your ministry" (2 Timothy 4:5).

- *Time to depart.* "For I am already being poured out as a drink offering, and the time of my departure has come" (2 Timothy 4:6).

- *Time for reward.* "I have fought the good fight, I have finished the course, I have kept the faith; in the future there is laid up for me the crown of righteousness, which the Lord, the righteous Judge, will award to me on that day; and not only to me, but also to all who have loved His appearing" (2 Timothy 4:7–8).

Paul urged Timothy to teach the word of God at all times—no matter what. The time was coming when men and women would not want the truth but would want a feel-good religion. Do we not see this time today in the Lord's church with Christians who want to hear what tickles their ears and not the profound truths found in God's precious Word?

What do we do today when people do not want to hear the true gospel? Do we change the gospel so that it will appeal to a wider group of people? No, we do not. Listen girls, we are *not* in the business of changing God's Word or Jesus' gospel. We stay the course; we endure the hardship; we fulfill the ministry God has given us just like Timothy was told to do. Above all, we must remember that our time to depart this life will arrive, and oh to be able to say like Paul, "I have fought the good fight, I have finished the course, I have kept the faith; . . . there is laid up for me the crown of righteousness."

A Horrible Day

Let's look at an amazing piece of published literature concerning September 11, 2001, a horrible time for Americans and for the world. I do not know who wrote it, but it was put on Facebook for all to read. When I read this, my heart is touched by these people who escaped death so innocently. They had no idea what that day would hold for them and the entire world.

Thanks for the Little Things

The head of a company survived 9/11 because his son started
    kindergarten.
Another man was alive because it was his turn to bring donuts.

One woman was late because her alarm clock didn't go
   off on time.
Another was late because of being stuck on the New Jersey
   turnpike because of an auto accident and his life was spared.
One missed his bus.
One spilled food on her clothes and had to take the time
   to change.
One's car wouldn't start.
One went back to answer the telephone.
One had a child that dawdled and didn't get ready as soon as he
   should have.
One couldn't get a taxi.
One man put on a new pair of shoes that morning. Before he got
   to the tower he developed a blister on his foot. He stopped at
   a drugstore to buy a bandage. That's why he is alive today.
Now when I am stuck in traffic, miss an elevator, turn back to
   answer a ringing telephone . . . all the little things that annoy
   me, I think to myself, "This is exactly where I'm meant to be
   at this very moment."

   —Facebook, unknown

MOMENTS IN PRAYER

Oh, precious Lord, thank You for the gift of time. Help us to use it wisely
and always use it for You. Please teach us patience in waiting for You and
Your time. May we never forget Your marvelous love in sending Jesus to
this earth. Help us to find the time for You today and every day. Please help
us to not be so selfish and self-absorbed. In Jesus' name, Amen.

Moments in Song

"Jesus Is All the World to Me" and "My Jesus, I Love Thee"

KEEP SEEKING

1. What does the word *time* mean to you?
2. How important was the timing for Jesus to come into the world? Discuss.

Timely Quotes

"Don't let yesterday use up too much of today."

—Will Rogers

"As the years pass, I am coming more and more to understand that it is the common everyday blessings of our common everyday lives for which we should be particularly grateful. They are the things that fill our lives with comfort and our hearts with gladness—just the pure air to breathe and the strength to breath it; just warmth and shelter and home folks; just plain food that gives us strength; the bright sunshine on a cold day; and a cool breeze when the day is warm."

—Laura Ingalls Wilder

"Lose not yourself in a far-off time, seize the moment that is thine."

—Friedrich Schiller

She's Come Undone

I was concerned . . . really concerned. Life in my family, the Fowler household, was rocking along, yes, but there was an unhealthy and distressing undercurrent flowing through our home—and nobody wanted to talk about it.

It was the winter of 1966. As a senior in high school, I was nearing the end of my high school experience, headed for the uncertainty of college life. All kinds of plans were buzzing around inside my head. Looking back on that time in my life, I now see that my precious family was walking on eggshells. I felt as restless as a cat on a hot tin roof.

Our home was just not as happy as it usually was. (Nobody has a perfect one!) Together, we had weathered many a storm and survived. The problem before us was Mom, our hub and our rock. Something was very wrong. It was she that was the real cat on a hot tin roof.

The missionary of all missionaries, Mom was unusual. Yes, she always supported my dad and helped him in his role as the preacher in the mission field of New England—a genuine preacher's wife. However, she was born to teach others the gospel of Jesus. She would go anywhere, anytime to teach anybody. Evangelism was simply in her blood.

The church work in Concord, New Hampshire, where we lived was demanding, challenging, exhausting, and wonderful. It is my "take" that when you are a missionary or in ministry, you are on call 24/7—the demands never stop. When I came home from school every day, it seemed there was always a car in the driveway and people inside, sitting around our kitchen table, studying the Bible with Mama. Sometimes it was a woman, crying, needing Mom's help. I remember one woman, in particular, who had so many problems. She was a single parent with five little children. I don't know how many times Mom would pull me aside and say, "Becky, you go take care of her kids while I see what is wrong." That is just the way it was.

Other times, Mom hopped into the car and drove to a new Christian's home, answering a cry for help. That is the way it worked with her. The phone rang; Mom answered and off she flew. Somebody needed Mama, and she was there. Our house was frequently full of guests, visitors from other states, oftentimes vacationing Christians or preachers and families who needed encouraging. Once again, Mom was instantly on task. My sister Judy and I ran to help her fix food, prepare the beds, and babysit the kids—we were her hands and feet. Stressed to the max? Oh, yes. But Mom could never say no. Sound familiar?

Living in Burnout

As you well know, stress can pile up enormously. It can even cause death! My precious mama needed to escape—to run away. Her body demanded rest and help—and lots of it! She had given to the point that she could not give any more. She was exhausted and on the verge of a nervous breakdown. But she couldn't stop, and she couldn't rest because there just was not any time to do that. And everybody needed Mama. I am sure she thought to herself, "Who else could do this but me?" But what she did not understand was that even the best of God's servants need help.

I know that my dad tried to help her, but he was at a loss too. She had no time for herself—no time for Lea. She was teetering at the brink of life's very edge—this is called "burnout."

One scene vividly stands out in my mind, as it was the weekend when things finally came to a head. A young preacher and his family from another state were spending the weekend with us. Naturally, Mom and Dad wanted to help them and encourage them in their work for the Lord. This couple had a little boy, two years old, who was completely out of control. The parents were totally oblivious to his whereabouts in our home and never restrained or disciplined him. Finally, the child discovered our piano. That was the straw that broke Mom's back.

You see, Mom was a musician, an excellent music teacher and piano teacher. We had always had a piano, and even as children, we were taught the piano was a special instrument and were never to mistreat it or abuse it. To pound on the piano was right up there with the blasphemy of the Holy Spirit—the unforgivable sin—absolutely forbidden and punishable by a slow, lingering death! Only a crazy person would pound on Lea Fowler's piano. And that small child was the epitome of crazy. He committed *the sin*. He stepped right up to that piano, rolled back the lid, and pounded the living daylights out of it. And pounded. And pounded. And neither of his parents made a move to stop him.

My sister and I tried to stop him. Mom tried to stop him. Once again, the lunatic parents never moved from their embrace on our comfy couch to deter or hinder their beloved offspring. Junior just kept on pounding.

That was it. That did it. I heard my mom, screaming and crying, fleeing to our basement where she could escape, not having to endure the circus in her living room. I had never in my life seen her fall apart like that. Never. And it lasted a very, very long time, as we could hear her weeping uncontrollably downstairs. Mom had finally come undone.

Furlough for the Fragile

I honestly don't remember what happened next. Suddenly the people were gone—thank the Lord! And they took that awful, crazy child home with them—hallelujah and amen! Parents, please, please don't let your children run amuck in other's homes. Be sensitive to those who have invited you. Discipline your children—for everybody's sake. How absolutely horrible and unforgivable it is to send the hostess over the edge!

Somehow life went on in our home, but we all knew that Mom was fragile. I was so worried about her. Perhaps you can relate to my story. Perhaps you know the feeling of watching someone you love falling down into a pit, and you are helpless. There is nothing you can do but watch and pray. I tried to help Mom—tried to talk to her and suggested getting help of some kind, but it was futile.

Then God stepped in. Our precious, precious God. Our omniscient, omnipotent, and omnipresent Father. Thank God for God! He always knows the right thing to do because He knows just what we need. Mom certainly needed divine intervention.

It was time for Mom and Dad to travel to a Christian college's lectureship, so off they went. I think they were gone for at least two weeks. Finally, they returned, and it was immediately clear that Mom was much better. She was happy, laughing, and loving—Lea was back! My mama had come home again.

When the moment presented itself, I was able to get her all to myself and ask the question I wanted to ask so badly. I pulled her aside and asked, "Mom, what happened? You are so much better."

She looked deep into my soul, knowing what I was really asking, and said, "Becky, I went to a class at the lectureship every day for a week. The teacher was so wonderful. You see, I had forgotten something."

"What?" I asked.

And Mom replied, "I had forgotten that God loves me."

Mom needed a break from the mission field where the work is tough. She needed a change of scenery, and she needed a vacation away from the constant demands of visitors, problems, and a constantly ringing telephone. But most of all, she needed God. She needed to immerse herself in His word and plumb its depths. She needed to put her burdens down and sit and learn at the feet of deeply spiritual and knowledgeable Christian teachers. So God provided that.

God Knows and Heals

As God's children, we do not always realize that God is at work in our lives and knows what is ahead—and how He will fix and deliver us. He is always there, observing everything and already working to prepare us for the problem that is going to devastate us ten years down the road. "For He looks to the ends of the earth and sees everything under the heavens" (Job 28:24).

I love this scripture from Psalm 68:19: "Blessed be the Lord, who daily bears our burden, the God who is our salvation." How often does God bear our troubles and woes? Daily. Every single day that we live. And don't forget the last line: "The God who is our salvation." It was God who was watching our mom and feeling her pain. Believe me, He was in our home the day that Mama fell over the edge, and I believe He caught her in His tender arms. I also believe our Master could feel our family's desperateness and inadequacy. Yes, it is true: Our God saves us. He certainly saved Mama, and in the process, He rescued our family.

God gives us these healing verses: "He restores my soul" (Psalm 23:3) and "The law of the Lord is perfect, restoring the soul" (Psalm 19:7).

Our Shepherd restores us, and the Word heals us. I call God "The Great Fixer" because He can fix anything and anybody. There is nothing He cannot do! Mom had become Humpty Dumpty, falling off the wall and breaking into multiple pieces. Who could really put Mom back together again? Only God. Who could heal her? Only the Great Physician who reached down from heaven and made her whole again.

Mom needed to plunge herself into God's precious Word and hear a whole week's worth about God's incredible love. Didn't she already know of His mighty love for her? Of course she did! But she needed to see it again in His Word. Like all of us, she had immersed herself in the need of the work at hand to the point that she had neglected her own spiritual needs. Like Mary, the sister of Martha, Mom needed to sit at Jesus' feet and let go of the "Martha duties" for a while. God stepped in, took Lea away, and restored her soul. And when the Father did this for my mama, the incredible teacher, she returned better than ever. She could teach again, help the lost find their way back to Him, and be our mom once more. God was not through with Mom yet. He had more work for her to do.

Thank God for the strong and biblical lectureships, seminars, sing-ings, and gospel meetings that avail themselves to anyone who wants to grow in the faith! We must never, never stop providing these events for the family of God. Don't you know that the Father sees to it that His children are surrounded by opportunities not only to be restored but to grow and walk with Him as well? But the question is: *Will His children find the time to meet Him there?*

Too often we are on the brink of collapse, and we don't do a thing about it. But we won't be any good to God and His work until we run away and embrace His love again. Let's wake up! Let's look around and escape to the spiritual mountain waiting for us!

Open your heart and let God work in it and on it. He will take you to a level of understanding you never thought possible.

Run away, my sister, run away. Why? You just may have forgotten that God loves you too.

Jeff and
Becky Blackmon

CHAPTER 4

Time for The House

Years ago my daughter Jenny and I were strolling around a popular antique mall when we encountered two signs displayed side by side. One sign read: "If Mama ain't happy, ain't nobody happy!" The other sign read: "If Daddy ain't happy, who cares?"

Jenny looked at me and said, "Oh Mom, that is so true!" We both collapsed with laughter. There is definite humor in this. Dad is the head of our home, and we absolutely adore him, but it is Mama who is the emotional and temperamental barometer in the family. Most families discover quickly that life is much more pleasant if Mom is singing in the kitchen . . . or at least singing somewhere.

A House for Visitors

Would you like to know what ticked my mom off instantly? I will let you in on our family secret because I saw it happen again and again. Yes, I am a slow learner, but I finally put two and two together on this. It all had to do with our "house." Here is the scene as it played out in the Fowler family house when I was growing up. We—the family—would drive home after an outing, get out of the car, and walk into the house. As soon as my mom saw a messy living room or an untidy kitchen, she would revert to a character we called "Sarge." Yes, she became a drill sergeant, immediately barking orders. We privates, along with Sarge, would "attack" whatever disorder was in front of us until it had disappeared. Then Sarge morphed back into Mama before our very eyes.

Believe me, Mom was not a neat freak with things having to be "just so." But she liked for clothes to be hung up, beds made, and the house straightened. If our bedroom was messy, she would say, "Just close the door." But she had one brilliant rule: The den or living room had to be straightened up before we went to bed because there just might be emergency guests arriving in the middle of the night. I can still hear her voice in my head, "Straighten up the front room. You just never know who is going to walk in the front door!" She was absolutely, unequivocally right, as we occasionally had a midnight visitor or two.

What unnerves you? Are there things in your house and life that cause you inner conflict? It is not at all unusual for us women to be unhappy with all kinds of matters, including ourselves. Many of us have low self-esteem issues, problems galore, and unhappy relationships. There are times that nothing makes us happy. But if Mama is unhappy all the time, the life of her family is completely miserable. Poor family.

Pause and Ponder

Take a moment and write down what makes you upset—housewise. Discuss in light of Titus 2:5.

The Dressing Room Experience

One desire of some women is to possess the figure of Julia Roberts, while having the appetite of Attila the Hun. We don't like ourselves or the image in the mirror that stares back at us. We don't like the way we look or our body shape. But we enjoy the eating moments that make our shapes.

We wish we were taller or shorter. We hate our clothes and our hair. It seems that all our friends are skinnier. It seems they are cute petite things while we may feel like a towering chunky Amazon from the jungle who wears size ten shoes and shops in the curvy girl's department.

We might hear others complain, "I just can't gain weight. I have to remind myself to eat!" Wouldn't you like to cause bodily harm to someone who says those words? I cannot tell you the many times I have been in the dressing room at a department store and heard something like this from the stall next door, "Mother, these jeans are too big! Can you see if you can find them in a size two!" (Size two? And jeans? Let me at her!)

I have to laugh though. After decades of trying on clothes and reliving the above scenario over and over, something happened recently that I thought would never happen in my lifetime. I was in a dressing room trying on something, and I heard the lady in the changing room next to me hissing to herself, "Fat, fat, fat!" I got a good chuckle out of that because I knew how that woman felt, felt, felt! Maybe you can identify too.

Our unhappy list goes on. We are not happy with our things. We want more. We want the prettier and bigger home on our street. It used to be that the American dream was to have a two-thousand-square-foot home. Now folks want more, much more.

Les Christie, in an article for CNN Money reports:

The average size of homes built last year [2017] hit 2,600 square feet, an all-time high that surpassed even the housing bubble years, when homes averaged around 2,400 square feet, according to the Census Bureau. . . . Meanwhile, extremely large houses—4,000 square feet and up—have been making up a much larger slice of the new homes built.[11]

We want new furniture and a snappy new car. We want more landscaping, more flowers, and a pool. We want more vacations and play dates. We also want what so-and-so has. Want, want, want. We are just not content.

There Is a Price

I once worked for a homemade cookie company that made daily "gift basket" deliveries all over our area. Occasionally, I made a few deliveries myself to help the company driver. I would approach the front door with a delivery and notice the tricycles on the lawn, revealing that young children lived there. As I rang the doorbell, I sometimes glanced in the window to see if anyone was coming to answer the door. Often the house inside was perfectly groomed and furnished to the hilt with the latest home décor, but there was no one home. Why? Because there is a price for having "breathtaking lifestyle." It requires a lot of money, at least two paychecks, and often another job.

When you set your heart on things, you will never be happy, and one thing you can count on will be the stress in your life. The apostle John was inspired to write these words to Christians:

> Do not love the world nor the things in the world. If anyone loves the world, the love of the Father is not in him. For all that is in the world, the lust of the flesh and the lust of the eyes and the boastful pride of life, is not from the Father, but is from the world (1 John 2:15–16).

My friend Ken used to ask me, "Are you old enough for your wants not to hurt you?" I didn't understand that old saying at first, but I do now.

Who Builds My House?

Somewhere along the line, when you grow up and have your own home—apartment, condo, brick house, or other dwelling—that place will reflect you. You are the woman in charge of that tangible dwelling.

I decorate my house with my tastes and preferences. Colors, curtains, furniture, and dishes. Have you ever walked into a friend's house and exclaimed, "Oh, this is so you"? You know what I mean. My house looks like me. And like my mom, I do not like for it to be a total disaster, although I don't mind a little disaster. When the room becomes too cluttered, I have to straighten it up and make it presentable before I am content again.

I realize now that when my mom fell apart because the house was a wreck, she reacted that way because it was her house—herself. She never wanted to look untidy any more than she wanted her house to look untidy. And if her house was messy, it meant that she was messy. We get that. So she had to fix her house immediately before she could function again.

But you have a spiritual house that surpasses this physical dwelling. Who builds that house? Who cares for that house?

Pause and Ponder

Write Psalm 127:1–2 here.

What is God telling us in this psalm from Solomon? As Brother Marshall Keeble used to say, "Let's handle it and see what we can get out of it."

The overall meaning here is: Unless the Lord builds and oversees the houses we are, inside and out, life is nothing. Unless the Lord is involved in every scene of our lives, life is a meaningless existence. Everything is empty if God is not there. The key to a wonderful life is to remember that God is in charge and we must yield to His authority.

With the words "unless the Lord builds," the psalmist asserts that life lived apart from God is not worth living, a view that this psalm shares with the book of Ecclesiastes. Even building a house is useless if the Lord is not in the process. The phrase, "the bread of sorrows," captures the essence of those removed from a sense of the Lord in their lives.[12]

King Solomon certainly repeats this theme in the book of Ecclesiastes. He continually states, "All is vanity." What does *vanity* mean? It means "a vapor, fleeting, just a breath, meaningless."

When we do not choose God to be our boss, we can only limp along on "painful labors," because God is not in charge. Life is empty so nothing goes right. To put it bluntly, life is a mess.

Burton Coffman comments, "The simple point is, that no matter how hard a man may work, if God's blessing is not upon him, it will all go for nothing."[13]

I cannot help but think of that hymn we sing, "Without Him" by Mylon LeFevre.

Isn't it true that we need Him for everything? Without Him we would surely fail.

Pause and Ponder

Research the song "Without Him" by Mylon LeFevre and either sing or say every word aloud. How are you inviting the Lord to build your spiritual house? Why do you need Him there?

Satan, the Master Liar

There is one who greatly desires to totally wipe out our house. What foolish women we would be if we really thought we would always have a happy-go-lucky, cheerio, "hi-ho, the derry-o" life, skipping about all day long with a dress, pearls, and high heels on! Life does not work that way. June Cleavers we are not. And the Christian life will never be that way—simply because we know that Satan is in the world and desires to kill us. Peter's inspired words prove that: "Be of sober spirit, be on the alert. Your adversary, the devil, prowls around like a roaring lion, seeking someone to devour" (1 Peter 5:8).

In my rush to understand who Satan is—as a roaring lion whose mission is to consume someone—I had not considered the first part of that verse enough. God adamantly warns all Christians to "be of sober spirit and be on the alert." What does that mean? God is warning His children to be sober: to be grave and solemn; to be serious about what the devil can do. Also to be on the alert: to watch and to look around us constantly. Why? Satan wants to take us captive. We must be on our toes to his wiles, his trickery, and his deceitful ways. His desire is to completely destroy us, our lives, our families, and our salvation. Someone has said: "The devil doesn't come to you with his red face and horns. He comes to you disguised as everything you've ever wanted."

John wrote at the end of his life: "We know that we are of God, and the whole world lies in the power of the evil one" (1 John 5:19). Yes, the whole world is in the hands of Satan.

Does Satan work on you in your life? He is constantly tempting me and trying to get my attention. Believe me, I am not "flip" or casual when it comes to his power. That is one thing I have learned as an older woman. I have seen him at work all these years in my life and in others' lives. I am of a sober spirit and I am on the alert.

Let me state right here that Satan will do everything he can to distract us, to destroy our house—every aspect of it—and fill us with his lies. The last thing he wants to see is a Christian with the right priorities. The very last thing the devil wants to encounter is a woman or man who loves God, obeys God, and lives for God.

> He was a murderer from the beginning, and does not stand in the truth because there is no truth in him. Whenever he speaks a lie, he speaks from his own nature, for he is a liar and the father of lies (John 8:44).

The devil will make us feel inadequate, ugly, and unloved. He is in that business. Daily he hurls beautiful models and their anorexic bodies with perfect hair, perfect makeup, and perfect wardrobe before our eyes, convincing us that is what we need to look like. All our insecurities kick in, along with discontentment, and Satan has a foothold in our life, especially in our house where we dwell. So we buy into the thinking that we need a bigger and different house, or we need more stuff to decorate our house/body. Then we are off on that demonic, materialistic pursuit, never to return. None of these things bring real happiness and contentment because these are fleeting things. Jesus had this to say about things:

> Beware, and be on your guard against every form of greed; for not even when one has an abundance does his life consist of his possessions (Luke 12:15).

> Do not store up for yourselves treasures on earth, where moth and rust destroy, and where thieves break in and steal. But store up for yourselves treasures in heaven, where neither moth nor rust destroys, and where thieves do not break in or steal; for where your treasure is, there your heart will be also (Matthew 6:19–21).

Time to Let the Savior In

All of us have asked ourselves, "How do I get the Lord's blessings in my life? How can I be happy? How can I build a good house? How do I receive God's magnificent love?" The answer is very simple. Choose God. Make Him your number one priority. Become a Christian. Wrap yourself up in the love of Jesus, inside and out. Put Him on the throne of your heart and let Him rule.

Has God left us in the dark about what He expects from us? Absolutely not. He tells us to hear, believe, repent, confess, and be baptized. Five easy steps. But that's not all. We must live for Him.

1. "So faith comes from hearing, and hearing by the word of Christ" (Romans 10:17).

2. "Therefore I said to you that you will die in your sins; for unless you believe that I am He, you will die in your sins" (John 8:24).

3. "Therefore having overlooked the times of ignorance, God is now declaring to men that all everywhere should repent" (Acts 17:30).

4. "And I say to you, everyone who confesses Me before men, the Son of Man will confess him also before the angels of God" (Luke 12:8).

5. "Repent, and each of you be baptized in the name of Jesus Christ for the forgiveness of your sins; and you will receive the gift of the Holy Spirit" (Acts 2:38).

How absolutely fabulous it is to have all our sins washed away, to be totally forgiven. I can still remember coming up out of the water and feeling so different. Can you? "Blessed are those whose lawless deeds have been forgiven, and whose sins have been covered" (Romans 4:7).

Pause and Ponder

Relate your own baptism story.

Why do you want God's blessings in your life?

Read Galatians 2:18–20 aloud. Underline these phrases in your Bible: "live to God," "no longer I who live," and "Christ lives in me."

The New House Is Ground Zero

When we are baptized, we become a completely new spiritual house. We have been converted—born again and changed. Like the Israelites who painted their houses with a perfect lamb's blood and were delivered, we have been washed and painted with Jesus' blood and delivered too. We even have a new name, Christian, which means "like Christ." Like Saul who became Paul, we make a 180-degree turn. Then we let God go to work on the house He wants us to be.

We have chosen God to be in charge now, and we have to do His will and not ours. We must play by His rules. We must obey Him if we want to succeed in anything. A preacher once said, "Obedience is doing what God says to do; how He says to do it; and when He says to do it."

Paul told the Ephesian church to "put on the new self" (Ephesians 4:22–24). When I became a Christian, I put off the old girl who wanted her way all the time and put on the new girl. I have to fight that old girl every day, because she wants to come up out of that grave. I have to stomp her right back down.

It is certainly true that if I do not choose God and obey Him, I—my house, myself—am a shaky old shack. God is my foundation; He surrounds me with His walls; He is in my heart and my mind. All these things describe the house I am now. I love God, and it is my desire to be that "beloved" who is blessed by God in Psalm 127:2, even when she sleeps! "For He gives to His beloved even in his sleep."

God Is the Architect

God is the architect; Jesus is the master carpenter, and we are the house that must be built anew. With them in charge of our life, our new house will be what they want, not what we want. We are not a structure that has to have a new window installed or a roof patched here and there, but we must raze our previous house and begin all over again—from the ground up.

My sweet sisters, please remember this: God is love and He loves us with an indescribable love. When we become His child, it's a win-win situation. We have peace and security no matter what happens, because He is in charge. How can we lose? Submission brings happiness into each day because pleasing God produces a happy life. We have chosen wisely. We have chosen to live righteously. That's the life to be lived, my sisters. Remember—if Mama ain't happy, ain't nobody happy. Perhaps you have heard the saying: Happy Wife, Happy Life! Sometimes when Jeff and I are having an argument, I ask him, "Do you want to be right or do you want to be happy?"

Our first concept is down: We are houses for God; we are new houses when we become Christians, and we want Him to build our spiritual houses. More concepts to follow, so don't go away, my sister. Let's meditate and let our minds dwell on these thoughts.

If today was my last day and tomorrow found me gone,
How would life be different, if that unknown somehow
    was known.
Would I be a better person, would I live a better life;
How much would I feed resentment, envy, bitterness, and strife?
How would I choose to live, and what would be my emphasis;
Being a blessing or a burden, full of service or selfishness?
Where would God be in my life, what place would He occupy,
If today was my last day, and before tomorrow I would die?
If today was my last day, and second chances all were through,
And I stood before my judge and my eternal fate I knew?
I would mourn and fall before Him, if I had not done what's right.
If I had chosen self and sin, if I had chosen eternal night.
But there's no reason for apprehension, I can die with
    head held high
If I die to self and live to Him, it won't matter when I die.

—Neal Pollard, used by permission

MOMENTS IN PRAYER

Oh Lord, help me to find the time for my house. Thank You so much
for this life and family You have given me. Help me, Lord, to obey
Your gospel and begin all over again. Please help me to find the time
to let You build my house. I love You. In Jesus' name, Amen.

Moments in Song

"Without Him I Would Be Nothing" and
"I Have Decided to Follow Jesus"

KEEP SEEKING

1. Describe your house.
2. What kind of house do you think God wants in you?
3. What does Satan want to do to your house, and what is he tempting you with right now?

Timely Quotes

"Marriage is like a deck of cards . . . In the beginning all you need is two hearts and a diamond. By
the end, you wish you had a club and a spade."

—Anonymous

"For what it's worth: It's never too late or, in my case too early to be
whoever you want to be. There's no time limit; stop whenever you
want. You can change or stay the same, there are no rules to this
thing. We can make the best or the worst of it. I hope you make the
best of it. And I hope you see things that startle you. I hope you feel
things you never felt before. I hope you meet people with a different
point of view. I hope you live a life you're proud of. If you find that
you're not, I hope you have the courage to start all over again."

—Benjamin Button, from the movie
The Curious Case of Benjamin Button screenplay by Eric Roth

"If you don't like something, change it. If you
can't change it, change your attitude."

—Maya Angelou

And the Lord Saved Them

In June of 2016 I had a car accident. It was quite jarring to say the least, but it was my fault. I had not checked my rearview mirror properly, and I hit an old pickup truck as I made a turn. I never saw the truck. I thought the insurance companies had settled the claim, but on July 11, everything changed. Here is what I wrote about that day.

July 11, 2016—I spent a lot of time today studying the book of Daniel and researching many aspects of his life. I rested. While fixing supper and thanking God for the quietness of the house and my love for just "being in the kitchen," Jeff came in and informed me of the certified letter to be picked up at post office. The letter was from an attorney who advertises about lawsuits. He was hired to defend the other party in the accident. Big ruthless lawyer deep in the heart of Texas.

My heart sank; Jeff and I prayed. I was sick. Finished supper, ate a little. Contacted my prayer warrior friends and asked them to pray. Kept reminding myself that we walk by faith and not by sight. Prayer warriors texted me with wonderful comforting words and scriptures to settle my soul. Checked Facebook and responded to old college friend's request to pray for her brother who was facing serious back surgery. Answered a text from a dear friend whose grandson is in rehab. Prayed for him and the family. "Things could be worse, Becky," I told myself.

Jeff and I began to read our Bibles together as we always do. We always read aloud together. From 1 Chronicles 11, Jeff had just finished reading the names of those brave and valiant men who served David—their heroism and their talents given to them by God: fearless Joab, Jashobeam who killed three hundred at one time; Eleazar who with David took a stand "in the midst of the plot [of barley] and struck down the Philistines; and the Lord saved them."

It was my turn to read, so I began:

Benaiah the son of Jehoiada, the son of a valiant man of Kabzeel, mighty in deeds, struck down the two sons of Ariel of Moab. He also went down and killed a lion inside a pit on a snowy day. He killed an Egyptian, a man of great stature five cubits tall. Now in the Egyptian's hand was a spear like a weaver's beam, but he went down to him with a club and snatched the spear from the Egyptian's hand and killed him with his own spear. These things Benaiah the son of Jehoiada did, and had a name as well as the three mighty men (1 Chronicles 11:22–24).

As I was reading, tears began falling on the pages of my Bible. I could see in my mind those men with David, standing in a barley field, fighting with all their strength, chopping down Philistines and barley at the same time. Barley and blood flying everywhere. The tears continued as I read aloud the accounts of Benaiah, who accomplished such great and mighty deeds for God's army of Israel. I imagined Benaiah, bravely plunging down into a pit on a cold snowy day, knowing God would deliver him from the lion below. And what was it like for him to attack a seven-and-a-half-foot-tall Egyptian armed with a long spear, grab it from him, and stab him with it?

I have always admired David and his ferocious band of brothers. Advisor Hushai once reminded David's son Absalom: "You know your father and his men, that they are mighty men and they are fierce, like a bear robbed of her cubs in the field. And your father is an expert in warfare" (2 Samuel 17:8).

And all I could think was how brave David and these men were and what a supreme coward I was. Walk by faith and not by sight? These men never gave it a thought. It was never an issue. They were thoroughly convinced of God's protection. They took their lives in their hands every single time they went to battle, but God delivered them each time. The Bible says that they "took their stand," and that is exactly what I wasn't doing. What was I afraid of? Where was my faith? If God could do these huge insurmountable feats through His children, couldn't He repeat them three thousand years later in the life of His child in Texas who was afraid of being sued?

The Bible simply states this fact, "And the Lord saved them" (1 Chronicles 11:14). And the Lord will save Becky. And the Lord will save you. He has done it before, and I know He will do it again. Have faith.

When I think of the powerful mighty God of the universe knowing my name and delivering me from the multiple crises in my life, I am absolutely humbled beyond description. I remember this question, quoted in both the Old and the New Testament: "What is man, that you take thought of [remember] him?" (Psalm 8:4; Hebrews 2:6). It truly leaves us feeling overwhelmed to be loved by God and delivered by God.

So many times I have felt the words expressed by a father in Mark 9:23–24 to be my words too. He came to Jesus with his demon-possessed son only to hear Him say, "All things are possible to him who believes." Immediately the boy's father cried out, "I do believe; help me in my unbelief."

The scene is so full of emotions, but it is the father who touches my heart the most. Mark tells us that the father immediately cried out to Jesus. I see the father saying these words as fast as he could and with as much urgency possible to convince Jesus that he believed and wanted his child healed. I see his eyes full of desperation as he tries to plead his case before the Savior. He had experienced years of trying to rescue his son from a very powerful demon. Without Jesus, this father had no hope at all. "I do believe . . . help me in my unbelief" or "Help me to believe more!" That is how I feel too. "Lord, help me to have more faith. Help me believe more, trust more, love more, study more, understand more, and pray more. Help me to be more. Help me to realize like that father, that without Jesus I have no hope at all!"

As we grow in the faith and grow in years, we will experience many tests, troubles, and woes. That's life. But being a Christian puts us on the inside track because God lives in us. Wasn't it Jesus who gave us this comfort scripture? "These things I have spoken to you, so that in Me you may have peace. In the world you have tribulation, but take courage; I have overcome the world" (John 16:33).

I don't know what crisis you are facing, my sister. But do this: Stop and give God the glory because He is at your side slaying the giants, decimating the woes in your life, and saving your soul, all at the same time. After all, He is God. We forget that. Why oh why are we so scared and fearful?

P.S. And the Lord saved Becky. No lawsuit. Oh Lord, You are my God and I will forever praise You! What is this girl that You remember her? Forgive me, O my Father, for my unbelief.

CHAPTER 5

Time to Jump Into the Deep End!

Okay, hold your nose, put your other hand up and jump. You are now in the deep end of the pool. Let's plunge and go really deep and look at another challenging passage about a "house."

> By wisdom a house is built, and by understanding it is established; and by knowledge the rooms are filled with all precious and pleasant riches (Proverbs 24:3–4).

It is time to let God build and establish your house. How will He build it and with what materials? Remember, you are a new house because you have become God's child, and old things have become new. Your sins are washed away. Also, your physical house, your body, will someday perish, but your spiritual house, your soul, will live on.

> Then the dust will return to the earth as it was, and the spirit will return to God who gave it (Ecclesiastes 12:7).

> For we know that if the earthly tent which is our house is torn down, we have a building from God, a house not made with hands, eternal in the heavens (2 Corinthians 5:1).

Time to Build the Spiritual House

The process of construction begins on our houses, our lives for Him. Where will we start? We must pour the foundation so that we will always be strong and stand for Him.

How often have we sung, "The Wise Man Built His House upon the Rock"? Countless times, especially if you attend VBS with your children or teach a children's class. Let's look at the two accounts of Jesus' teachings about this house.

> Therefore everyone who hears these words of Mine and acts on them, may be compared to a wise man who built his house on the rock. And the rain fell, and the floods came, and the winds blew and slammed against that house; and yet it did not fall, for it had been founded on the rock. Everyone who hears these words of Mine and does not act on them, will be like a foolish man who built his house on the sand. The rain fell, and the floods came, and the winds blew and slammed against that house; and it fell—and great was its fall (Matthew 7:24–27).

Pause and Ponder

Read Luke 6:46–49 aloud. What word describes the rain?

Have you ever analyzed and meditated on the "Wise Man" song? Is Jesus telling us how to construct a physical dwelling? Absolutely not. This house represents a person like us who has a choice to obey or disobey God. The wise woman is the woman who chooses God and builds herself, her faith, her very being on the words of Jesus.

From reading the two accounts from Luke and Matthew, does anything jump out at you? What I notice right off is that the building of a strong house or of a weak house is predicated on the basis of obedience to Jesus. Look again. "Everyone who comes to Me, hears My words, and walks away?" No, Jesus didn't say that. He said, "and acts on them." To act on His words is to obey Him—simple, plain, and to the point.

We read aloud the words "dug deep" from Luke 6:48. If we want a strong foundation in our houses, we must dig deeply and build ourselves on Jesus. And this takes time—and blood, sweat, and tears. We are the houses that will never collapse because we are built on our Savior and His marvelous words. He is our rock and our strength.

> This is the key to the paragraph. People who build upon Jesus' words build upon the solid rock; people who build upon anything else are doomed to disappointment. The word of Christ alone is the constitution of the church, the ground of eternal hope, the guide of faith, the source of redemption, and the true wisdom of God. All else is shifting sand. . . . If men indeed hope to receive eternal life, they must receive it of Christ and upon the terms laid down by him.[14]

The child of God has quite a task, doesn't she? In yielding to Jesus, she builds herself wisely, comprehends the importance of her task, and fills her being with the knowledge that comes from God, not the world. She is seeking the precious moments.

As Christian women, we are daughters of the King and that is serious business. With the Bible as our foundation, how can we go wrong? The Bible has all the answers to living righteously and making it to heaven.

> Seeing that His divine power has granted to us everything pertaining to life and godliness, through the true knowledge of Him who called us by His own glory and excellence (2 Peter 1:3).

The words, "everything pertaining to life and godliness," are adequate when describing our Christian lives. God has given us everything to help us live this life and live it godly. Everything—daily challenges, raising the kids, getting along with the brethren, sharing the gospel, breathing, dying, and all the stuff in between—is covered in the Bible. My preacher friend Steve says, "If we can't do it God's way, don't do it!"

We must never stop loving God's words, absorbing them, and taking them into our hearts. And when we act on them, we are rock solid, strong houses, living for God, and not falling for anything. We even have peace in our lives. David, that wonderful psalmist, described it: "Those who love Your law have great peace, and nothing causes them to stumble" (Psalm 119:165).

When your house is built upon a rock, you can withstand anything because Jesus is your foundation. Whatever storm comes your way, you will survive because your house is built on God. When doctrinal error comes your way, you will not fall for that either. How does that old saying go? "If you don't stand for something, you'll fall for anything."

Precious Moments of Forgiveness

Obeying the gospel is the genesis of our faith—the beginning. What if I goof up and sin again? Am I lost forever? Is my house destroyed? No. Pray and ask for forgiveness. Determine to do better. We must be faithful to God and never leave His side.

Romans 3:23 says, "All have sinned and fall short of the glory of God." We are forgiven of past sins, but we know realistically that we can sin every day. Do we keep being baptized every day? No, we don't have to do that.

> If we say that we have fellowship with Him and yet walk in the darkness, we lie and do not practice the truth; but if we walk in the Light as He Himself is in the Light, we have fellowship with one another, and the blood of Jesus His Son cleanses us from all sin. If we say that we have no sin, we are deceiving ourselves and the truth is not in us. If we confess our sins, He is faithful and righteous to forgive us our sins and to cleanse us from all unrighteousness (1 John 1:6–9).

That passage is written in continual present tense: "Walk" means "keep on walking." This "walking" metaphor means to stay faithful to God and obey Him in all things. When we Christians sin, we ask for forgiveness, and God forgives because "we have an advocate with the Father, Jesus Christ the righteous. He is the propitiation for our sins"

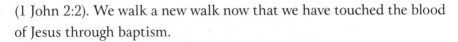

(1 John 2:2). We walk a new walk now that we have touched the blood of Jesus through baptism.

> Or do you not know that all of us who have been baptized into Christ Jesus have been baptized into His death? Therefore we have been buried with Him through baptism into death, so that as Christ was raised from the dead through the glory of the Father, so we too might walk in newness of life (Romans 6:3–4).

In Jesus, through Jesus, and because of Jesus we are God's children, forgiven and sanctified. Abide in Him, cherish time with Him, and keep His words. Walking with Him demands our precious moments.

Pause and Ponder

Why is it so time consuming to "walk in newness of life"?

Live Here and Sin Less

Do you sometimes wish for a sanctuary where you are protected from sin? Examine John's inspired words:

> I am the vine, you are the branches; he who abides in Me and I in him, he bears much fruit, for apart from Me you can do nothing. If anyone does not abide in Me, he is thrown away as a branch and dries up; and they gather them, and cast them into the fire and they are burned. If you abide in Me, and My words abide in you, ask whatever you wish, and it will be done for you. My Father is glorified by this, that you bear much fruit, and so prove to be My disciples. Just as the Father has loved Me, I have also loved you; abide in My love. If you keep My commandments, you will abide in My love; just as I have kept My Father's commandments and abide in His love. These things I have spoken to you so that My joy may be in you, and that your joy may be made full (John 15:5–11).

The Greek word *meno* is translated "abide," "continue," and "remain" in our English text. Jesus is the true vine, our source of strength and nourishment. When we hold on to Him and abide in His instructions constantly, not only do we make Him joyful, but we ourselves know true joy as well. When we make God happy, then we are happy too.

Pause and Ponder

Circle the word *abide* in the text above. How is your life better when you follow Jesus' instructions? What is the consequence of being apart from Him?

Don't Look Back!

Praise God that restoration and forgiveness are easy with such a wonderful Father. But it is crucial to keep right on walking with the Lord and never look back. That is the saved state. Our eyes are on heaven, and earth holds no power over us. Can we relate to Paul's sentiments?

> Brethren, I do not regard myself as having laid hold of it yet; but one thing I do: forgetting what lies behind and reaching forward to what lies ahead, I press on toward the goal for the prize of the upward call of God in Christ Jesus (Philippians 3:13–14).

To willfully leave the Lord and go off on our own pursuits is like taking our souls camping in a danger zone. Satan tempts us with worldly lusts to entice us to sin and give up on God. He makes sin look like fun. He loves it when a Christian absents herself from worship. And it certainly is true that the longer one stays away from God, the easier it becomes.

The longer we serve Satan, the longer we are away from our Father. Any minute spent away from the presence of God is sixty seconds too long. The longer we stay away from worship, fellowship, and personal Bible study, the more worldly we become and the more worldly our houses become. Doesn't that make sense? Someone wisely stated, "The more we miss church, the less we miss church."

My Psalms

I am thankful that God forgives the way He does. Many times my God, in His overwhelming mercy, has dealt with me as a child and lovingly guided me back to the right path. Don't we sometimes make foolish choices? I know that I certainly have!

Words are inadequate to describe God's love for me and mine. If not for God's love, where would I be? I doubt that I would be alive. Can anybody relate? I believe David felt that way too. Let this verse touch your soul: "If the Lord had not been my help, my soul would soon have dwelt in the abode of silence" (Psalm 94:17).

If the Lord had not loved us, where would we be? We would be like those in Judges who did what was right in their own eyes—lost! How thankful I am for my Father's unrelenting mercy, kindness, and forgiveness. I will praise Him as long as I breathe. "Because Your loving-kindness is better than life, my lips will praise You, so I will bless You as long as I live" (Psalm 63:3–4).

Scripture tells us that God is eager to forgive. I call Psalm 86:5 the "good and ready" verse. "For You, Lord, are good, and ready to forgive, and abundant in lovingkindness to all who call upon You."

We need to be that way too. Dan Winkler said it well: "Forgiveness is the gift that keeps on giving." God has forgiven us over and over, and we must do likewise—over and over.

Pause and Ponder

Comment on the following statement by C. S. Lewis: "To be a Christian means to forgive the inexcusable because God has forgiven the inexcusable in you."

The Sweet Strong Psalm

Have you read Psalm 1? Did you know that it is the second most popular psalm, Psalm 23 being the most popular? It only has six verses, so let's stop, open our Bibles, and read together.

Now reread it and substitute "woman" for "man" and "her" for "his." It makes it sound so much more personal for us women. *Blessed* means "happy." Happy is the woman who . . .

1. *How blessed is the [woman] who does not walk in the counsel of the wicked, nor stand in the path of sinners, nor sit in the seat of scoffers* (Psalm 1:1). Here is a description of the woman of God who does not walk, stand, or sit contrary to God. Satan wants the Christian woman to surround herself with wicked people and scoff at God's law. What does *scoff* mean? It is to mock, to jeer, to make fun of. Have you ever known a person who mocked God or spiritual things? We know what happens when we surround ourselves with mockers and scoffers; we become just like them. Scoffers are negative people, and negativism is contagious.

2. *But [her] delight is in the law of the Lord, and in His law [she] meditates day and night.* The woman of God is happy; she loves the Book. How much? To the point that she thinks, contemplates, and muses constantly about His words. God is her top priority. His precious Word is with her continually because she is in the Word continually. *Hagah,* the Hebrew word for *meditate,* means "to ponder, study, and talk." Apply this description of the blessed woman in this psalm. She studies the law, thinks about the law, and talks about the law because that is her world. She is God's woman. That is who I want to be.

3. *[She] will be like a tree firmly planted by streams of water, which yields its fruit in its season and its leaf does not wither; and in whatever [she] does, [she] prospers.* Take note of this person likened to a tree. It's rooted, strong, and fruitful. Why? Because she delights in the law of God.

It does not take a rocket scientist to figure out that if we read and study our Bibles, we will be strong in the faith, happy, blessed, and bearing fruit for the kingdom of God.

4. *The wicked are not so, but they are like chaff which the wind drives away.* My desire is to be that sturdy tree and not like the stubble which flies away. I want to be that woman, a woman who has dug deeply and built herself on the rock of Jesus, a woman whose roots are so strong that she stands firmly no matter the storm, a woman that my God can depend on.

I have chosen God to be in charge of every single thing in my life. He is the one who builds my house, and He knows best. I must do His will, play by His rules, and obey Him to live with Him in heaven. It's worth repeating, "Obedience is doing what God says to do; how He says to do it; and when He says to do it!"

My sisters, we are going to continue our discussion about our minds and our "house." Stay in the deep end with me.

No Time

I knelt to pray but not for long;
I had too much to do.
I had to hurry and get to work,
For bills would soon be due.

So I knelt and said a hurried prayer,
And jumped up off my knees.
My Christian duty was now done,
My soul could rest at ease.

All day long I had no time
To spread a word of cheer;
No time to speak of Christ to friends;
They'd laugh at me I feared.

No time, no time, too much to do,
That was my constant cry;
No time to give to souls in need,
But at last the time to die.

And when before the Lord I came,
I stood with downcast eyes.
For in His hands God held a book;
It was the book of Life.

God looked into His book and said,
"Your name I cannot find.
I once was going to write it down,
But never found the time."

—Author unknown

MOMENTS IN PRAYER

Oh, Father, thank You for the book of Psalms and the way it changes us. Help us to be good children who love You and follow Your commandments. Lord, please help us to seek the precious moments to be the blessed woman of Psalm 1. In Jesus' name, Amen.

Moments in Song

"My Hope Is Built on Nothing Less" and "Give Me the Bible"

KEEP SEEKING

1. How does 2 Corinthians 5:17 relate to our "spiritual house"?

2. Have you ever built a house from the ground up or known someone who has? Describe the experience.
3. How important is it to study the Old Testament?
4. How do you know that the God of the Old Testament is the same as the God of the New Testament?

 Timely Quotes

"The fact that I am a woman does not make me a different kind of Christian, but the fact that I am a Christian makes me a different kind of woman."

—Elisabeth Elliot

"One day is worth a thousand tomorrows."

—Benjamin Franklin

"The most important of the Lord's work you will ever do will be the work you do within the walls of your own home."

—Harold B. Lee

A Sentimental Journey

Would you be surprised if I told you that cooking can be thought provoking, even emotional and life changing? Well, it can. The very act of planning a menu, finding a recipe, and even delivering a baked, grilled, or sautéed product to the table can be filled with laughter, memories, and delight.

Let me explain. I needed a recipe for taco salad, or "Mexican Stack Up," as it is known around these parts. Some cooks are able to go to their index cards and notebooks and find immediately the recipe they need. Not this old girl. My recipe box is incomplete and stuffed. If I am unable to locate a recipe, I begin to look in odd places, one of which is a brown paper bag with handles. Before you chuckle, let me add that this particular paper bag is a *fancy* paper bag. That makes it better, right?

In the recipe bag are many of my precious culinary delights, written on recipe cards, lined paper, stationery, sticky notes, and what have you. There is also a conglomeration of handwriting, all from friends and relatives, no enemies allowed. And do I need to mention that most of these pieces of precious parchment are soiled and covered with grease or food spots? (True signs of deliciousness.)

I smiled as I glanced quickly through the cookies and cakes. I've got a thing for sugar and casseroles. Then I noticed the personal notes written along with many of the culinary formulas. "Bring to the church building by 2:00 PM" or "Sure do love you!"

I looked fondly at the recipes from some important women in my life who have passed on. There was Sister Hayes' "Lemon Cake" from Tennessee and Miss Lucy's "Jerome Cookies" from Georgia. I remembered their faces, hospitality, and humorous ways.

I saw the handwriting of family members who have died, and it touched my soul. I glanced at my precious father-in-law's neat printing of "Vidalia Onion Pie" and his favorite, "Apple Cake." This made me stop and remember his unique sense of humor. I smiled to myself, but my heart hurt too.

I saw an old, worn, spotted, folded piece of typing paper, and I knew what it was before I even opened it. Mom's "Turkey and Dressing" recipe had been hastily written for me, a young bride some forty-six years ago. I gently unfolded it, and I could feel her personality spill over into her quick message: "Dear Beck, Don't really have time to write. Jan baptized today. Having about twenty-three in tomorrow for preachers' meeting. (Counting children.) Speak in Seabrook Tues."

A quick message. Even quicker recipe and instructions. But a distinct personality and a lifetime of memories in that one piece of paper.

Was it her recipe that was touching? No, it was the information before it. Happenings in their mission work in New England took top priority, as they should. A baptism, a fellowship, and time for encouragement with other missionaries. A talk to encourage women. All at the top of the list. Then food. Real food before physical food.

I have to admit, I smiled through the tears as I made my journey through those recipes. I found the needed taco salad recipe—in my mother's organized recipe box, of course, not in my messy menagerie of culinary favorites. Maybe I needed to find "her" once more before I found "it."

A recipe is an excursion of memories, a junket of summer picnics, dinners on the ground, and family gatherings trapped in our head. Messages from the past appear magically before us in a loved one's handwriting. Precious, precious memories.

What started out as a search for a spicy recipe ended up as a sweet trip down memory lane. But this time there was something more. What began as a quest for a formula became a reminder of bottom-line Christian living. Jesus said in Matthew 28:19–20, "Go therefore and make disciples of all the nations, baptizing them in the name of the Father and the Son and the Holy Spirit, teaching them to observe all that I commanded you; and lo, I am with you always, even to the end of the age." The Great Commission flowed out of Jerusalem two thousand years ago and is still every Christian's marching orders.

Oh, my little chickens, God in His incredible nature orchestrates and moves in our lives so magnificently that He can stop us and teach us volumes about true Christianity even in the simplest of ways. All I wanted was to find a taco meat recipe. I think my Father was pleased that I learned three very important lessons: the fields are white unto harvest, the workers need to be encouraged, and women need one another. What started out as a simple search for food turned into a sentimental journey and a sober reminder of what life is all about. It's about Him, and it always will be.

How amazing our Father is! What is He doing in your life on a daily basis? He is full of surprises. Who would have imagined that one could find the Lord's mighty lessons in a wrinkled up brown paper bag?

6

Time To Fill 'Er Up!

Have you heard the old joke about how you can tell if a woman is a true southern belle? She gets a credit card in the mail in the morning, and by 4:00 PM the numbers are worn slap off!

Oh, how true. If you can relate and you are from another part of the world, you are a bonafide, deep down, southern belle. You just didn't know it.

For most of us women, the allure of shopping is strong. I know there are some females who detest shopping, but I believe the majority like to spend money and decorate. Perhaps God put our love for decorating in those XX chromosomes.

The Home of Fixer Upper

At the writing of this book, Jeff and I live in the great metropolis of Waco, Texas. If you are a fan of Home and Garden Television (HGTV), you automatically know about the Gaines family. Chip and Joanna Gaines have turned this little city upside down with their show, "Fixer Upper." For some five seasons, this dynamic duo has helped people find a home, tear up that home, and then rebuild it. In today's lingo, this is called flipping a house. Chip is the muscles, tearing the old house down and building it back up again. Joanna is the brains, designing and decorating the new house inside and outside.

Their show has been a huge hit in America, even reaching first place in viewers' homes. It has been refreshing to see a couple work together who not only love one another but also have four happy children—and a new baby. Part of the appeal of "Fixer Upper" has been the emphasis on a normal home—mom, dad, and the kids. When was the last time we had that kind of family on a weekly TV series?

Furthermore, Waco has reaped the benefits of the Gaines' popularity, as thousands travel from all over the United States to visit their shops. The statistics are staggering: some 30,000 tourists visit weekly. Yes, weekly. And if there is local special event, like a Food Truck Contest, the number of visitors can reach 350,000.

The Silos—the Gaines' shop situated by old grain silos in the heart of town—is chock-full of items that bring all kinds of glamor to one's home. Rugs, chandeliers, flowers, vases, pictures, table decorations, plates, and more fill the shelves and walls. A plethora of beautiful things, all with hefty price tags, tempt shoppers. Items fly off the shelves because most women love Joanna Gaines' style, want to imitate it, and will pay anything to get it.

What Will I Choose to Fill My House?

Just as we have to shop and find the things that make our physical home more attractive, pleasant, and livable, think about how we can fill our spiritual brain with pleasant riches. Remember our previous thoughts about the house we are building? Remember "The Wise Man Built His House Upon the Rock"? We have found the foundation and built that house. What comes next? The house must be filled with the "right stuff."

> By wisdom a house is built, and by understanding it is established; and by knowledge the rooms are filled with all precious and pleasant riches (Proverbs 24:3–4).

My spiritual house is the dwelling place of my heart, and I am responsible for filling it with wonderful treasures. What kind of treasures? Gold, silver, precious expensive things? Expensive pleasures? No, those things are fleeting and empty. It is the godly things that are the precious and pleasant riches, not the lamps, rugs, or chandeliers.

Matthew Henry was an English non-conformist clergyman best known for his commentary, *Exposition of the Old and New Testaments,* written in 1710. He had this to say about Proverbs 24:3–4: "Piety and prudence in outward affairs, both go together to complete a wise man. By knowledge the soul is filled with the graces and comforts of the spirit, those precious and pleasant riches."[15]

Pause and Ponder

What did Jesus have to say about trusting in and saving treasures? Memorize Matthew 6:19–21.

Beyond DNA

Does the Bible have answers about pursuing materialism and forgetting about God? Consider Solomon's wisdom,

> He has made everything appropriate in its time. He has also set eternity in their heart, yet so that man will not find out the work which God has done from the beginning even to the end (Ecclesiastes 3:11).

Now let's handle this passage and see what we can get out of it. It is God who is the "He." God has created everything appropriate—*appropriate* meaning "beautiful."

"Man will not find out the work which God has done." Will we ever understand and know God's work? No, it is impossible because we do not have the mind of God.

Now let's pluck the middle sentence out of the verse: "He has also set eternity in their heart." Whose heart? Mankind's heart. What does this mean?

Here is what Ol' Beck thinks. Have you ever really wanted something you saw while shopping? Perhaps it was an outfit or a piece of furniture. You finally were able to bring the outfit home or a truck delivered the furniture. And neither the outfit nor the furniture excited you like you thought it would. Where did the love and initial excitement go? What happened? I wrote about it in *The Begging Place*:

> There is an emptiness inside you because you thought having that dress or that dining room set was going to bring you joy. You are not as happy as you thought you would be. . . . The reason the outfit or the furniture did not bring you happiness is because things are just that: things. Things do not bring you happiness because God has placed eternity in your heart. The spiritual void in our hearts cannot be satisfied with things. . . . Try as we will, we can never make the shallow things of this earth fill that void in our hearts. We will never be happy with material things because God has created man to want Him. When we put God in our hearts and minds, that's substance! The void starts to fill up and we feel better. We can grow on that.[16]

Only God can fill that void in our heart called eternity. Only He can fit. Why? Because He has created us to discover our need for Him. The entire world is on a quest to discover happiness, but few will realize that a house filled with God is genuine happiness. We can run but we cannot hide from our "eternity" in our hearts. God made us. This is beyond DNA.

Don't Run on Empty

We must fill heads and minds with spiritual things: reading and studying the Bible, prayer, godly living, good recreation, kind thoughts, and such like. These are the riches and treasures in our rooms. Are there more treasures and furnishings to add to our house? The Lord never leaves us in the dark regarding our spiritual growth. But how in the world are we going to know what God wants from us, expects from us, and what kind of life He desires for us if we never open His Book? Phil Sanders said it so well, "When our minds and our hearts stop studying the word of God and start listening to the worldly pleasures, we lose sight of God and we begin to follow the world."

I agree with this quote from A. W. Tozer: "The more fascinated we become with the toys of this world, the more we forget that there's another world to come."

Let's be honest with ourselves and look at our priorities. Let us be aware and be constantly heedful of what we have set our minds upon. Do we open His Book and say, "Fill me up"? Are we thinking of God, pleasing Him and living for Him, or are we thinking of ourselves, our own wants and desires? I can still hear Mom quoting Luke 12:15 to me as I became an adult, "For a man's life does not consist in the abundance of his possessions."

What consumes every waking moment? God has given us these eye-opening verses in Romans 8:5–8:

> For those who are according to the flesh set their minds on the things of the flesh, but those who are according to the Spirit, the things of the Spirit. For the mind set on the flesh is death, but the mind set on the Spirit is life and peace, because the mind set on the flesh is hostile toward God; for it does not subject itself to the law of God, for it is not even able to do so, and those who are in the flesh cannot please God.

Make a List, Check It Daily

Let's look at a few marvelous lists where God gives us further instructions. Observe the qualities God desires to see in our lives.

- *The Fight List*—"Pursue righteousness, godliness, faith, love, perseverance, and gentleness. Fight the good fight of faith; take hold of the eternal life to which you were called, and you made the good confession in the presence of many witnesses" (1 Timothy 6:11–12).

- *The Fruit List*—"But the fruit of the Spirit is love, joy, peace, patience, kindness, goodness, faithfulness, gentleness, self-control; against such things there is no law" (Galatians 5:22–23).

- *The Virtue List*—"Now for this very reason also, applying all diligence, in your faith supply moral excellence, and in your moral excellence, knowledge, and in your knowledge, self-control, and in your self-control, perseverance, and in your perseverance, godliness, and in your godliness, brotherly kindness, and in your brotherly kindness, love. For if these qualities are yours and are increasing, they render you neither useless nor unfruitful in the true knowledge of our Lord Jesus Christ. For he who lacks these qualities is blind or short-sighted, having forgotten his purification from his former sins" (2 Peter 1:5–9).

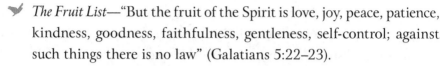

Pause and Ponder

- Talk about each of these lists. Underline them in your Bible. Compare them. Discuss them. Pray about them, and put them into your life.

- Underline qualities from the lists above that are your strengths. Circle the ones you need to work on.

Wise Mama Moments

Please remember this: We mamas set the tone of our house. If we love the Lord and serve Him, we cannot stop talking about Him to our entire family. Why wouldn't any mama share the Lord constantly with her children and husband? Don't we all want to get to heaven with our family? Not only will our "houses" shout what is important to us, but our family will daily see Christ living in us.

Other than Jesus, Mama is the most important teacher we will ever know. What we mamas say and do speaks volumes to all, especially our offspring. Our children and grandchildren will see the importance of knowing God and obeying Him. We will point out God's mighty and powerful hand as He delivers all of us in different situations and teaches us important life lessons—from the passing of a Spanish test to the passing of a temptation Satan has sent our way.

Oh, my sisters, never keep quiet about the Lord! To be silent about heaven and hell is a trait of a foolish woman. The Lord had this to say about a foolish woman: "The wise woman builds her house, but the foolish tears it down with her own hands" (Proverbs 14:1). We either build up our home or we tear it down. Wise or foolish, what will it be?

Keeping one's mouth shut about God is exactly what Satan wants but not what God wants. Satan, not God, is in the timidity, scaredy-cat business. "For God has not given us a spirit of timidity, but of power and love and discipline" (2 Timothy 1:7).

If God has not given us a spirit of timidity—if God has not made us fearful, then who has? That's easy. It is Satan. God gives us power, love, and self-control. We can do anything because God gives us the power. However, the devil loves to make us feel weak and timid. And when we buy into being timid, we don't speak up about our faith and what Jesus has done for us.

What do we talk about with our family? What's the chatter in our house about? If we are concerned with money, sports, shopping, and material things, those are the treasures filling the rooms of our house. They are our focus and the main topic of conversations. Our focus comes out of our mouths. Jesus described this in Matthew 15:18 when He said, "But the things that proceed out of the mouth come from the heart." He further said in Matthew 6:21, "For where your treasure is, there will your heart be also."

Either way there will be no doubt what our house stands for. The moments with our family, the words that we speak, and the love we give away are the elements—the walls, bricks, and mortar—that define us.

This time, these words, this love is what our family remembers. Thomas Aquinas once wrote, "The things we love tell us what we are."

How will we be remembered, mamas? Only you and I know the legacy we are leaving those we love. Why? Because we know what our house is made of and what it is filled with. We know our house from room to room.

How Do I Fill My Rooms?

Think about it. We want our house to be filled with God, so we must seek the precious moments for God. What about memorizing scriptures from God's Word? Isn't it a great idea to have a room in our head that recalls memorized verses? Can we do it? Of course we can. Select a memory verse a month; write it down, and post it around the house. Stop and say it several times a day. Cherish it. Yes, it is harder to memorize as we get older, but let's try to keep the brain working and watch God help us. Trust me on this. We know more scriptures from the Bible than we think we do.

Keep a notebook handy so that you can take notes during the Bible class and worship. You will get much more out of the Bible classes and worship if you do that. God has much to teach us, and a lot of it is learned throughout the years of faithful church attendance. You will hear the same passages taught over time, and before you know it, you are quoting them. And you are so proud of yourself for remembering.

There is something powerful about taking notes of sermons that help your faith grow. Confucius once said, "I hear and I forget. I see and I remember. I do and I understand." Simply stated, you get the picture when you take notes. And your notebook and pen will be handy to write the names and addresses of visitors or those in need of prayer.

These actions fill your rooms with treasures. Someone has said, "At some point it has to go from being highlighted in our Bibles to being written on our hearts."

God's Word is and will always be the biggest treasure we shall ever know. Be a pearl seeker. Seeking precious moments of study and meditation is the way to grow in the faith. It is living the inspired words of Peter: "But grow in the grace and knowledge of our Lord and Savior Jesus Christ" (2 Peter 3:18). And don't forget, your children are watching you and imitating you. I cannot remember a worship service when my mom did not take notes. If she didn't have a notebook, she dug in her purse and found a used envelope or a grocery store receipt.

Commit to God to read His Word every day. These are your precious moments. Don't let a single day go by without opening up the Book and focusing your eyes on words spoken from Him to you. God fashioned our brains so magnificently to remember. Our minds are more powerful than we realize. Also, keep in mind that God always has a plan for our walk with Him. He knows just what we need. Here is a great scripture to prove this: "So will My word be which goes forth from My mouth; It will not return to Me empty, without accomplishing what I desire, and without succeeding in the matter for which I sent it" (Isaiah 55:11).

Our sweet sister, Jane McWhorter, wrote these magnificent words in her book about memories, *Roses in December*:

> Just as a baby needs to kick and exercise his leg muscles in order to be able to walk one day, so do we need to exercise our spiritual muscles if we are to develop into the kind of children God wants us to be.[17]

My sisters, don't keep God in a box. Let Him out. Let Him do the work He needs to do in our houses, but first we must do our part. Let's get into the Word and memorize what we can. Let's take notes and broaden our spiritual education and maturity. Our Almighty God and Father is always watching and waiting to bless us. He is the one we want to make happy—not Visa!

Finding the Treasures

Jeff and I have read through the Bible every year for the past four years. We are using a great reading schedule which includes a reading from the Old Testament, the New Testament, a Psalm, and a Proverb. We read four to six chapters a night. Although we were always daily Bible readers, it was even better when we decided to read together out loud. Jeff reads a chapter, then I read a chapter. We divvy up the reading and often stop and ask, "What does this mean? Who is talking?" Together we have grown in our love for God. Following this program takes a lot of dedication, and we've found that if we skip a chapter or two occasionally, catching up takes quite a bit of time. If we are separated overnight, we take the reading schedule with us, so as not to fall behind.

It breaks my heart that few Christian couples read their Bibles, out loud, together. In fact, I do not know of another couple who does this. When I ask my sisters if they read the Bible with their husbands, many of them say to me, "Becky, I wish my husband would read with me, but he won't." I will never understand why a man who loves God will not read the Bible aloud with His wife. Let's pray about that.

The Sisters

Seek out the treasures called "sisters." Go to ladies' Bible class. You will find yourself in a company of women who want to know more about God while being together. You will laugh together and cry together, but most of all, you will grow in your love for God and for one another. Many women have commented, "I don't know what I would do without my sisters." "Oh, the prayer warriors in our class!" "It is the women there who understand me."

Oh, my sisters, love one another; attend the ladies' Bible class and learn. Don't be afraid of one another. Get to know the sister who is unfamiliar or even scary to you. Make her your friend. You just may find a mentor, an older woman who can help you in a crisis. Fill your life and soul with wonderful godly women. Study the book *Side by Side* by Brenda Poarch to hone your skills in developing Christian friendships. Trust me, God will send you the women you need to grow spiritually.

Seek opportunities that God gives for us to grow. Go to that lecture-ship you have heard about, take notes, and write down the good things that helped you to mature in the faith. Share your notes with others and open the prospect of more discussion with someone. Travel to a gospel meeting, and you will find that God is already waiting for you to arrive and receive the blessings of singing, praying, and hearing a great message. A visiting preacher will often challenge me with a scripture I never understood, and it is always thrilling to grasp that concept. That was all in God's plan. God knew it all the time, and Satan did everything he possibly could to keep me from attending that meeting.

Check out the book displays at seminars. Start your own library of spiritual materials that will not only help you but also your family and others. Buy the books that will help to expand your own brain and help you to become a better Christian. Then reach for that spiritual book or Christian magazine instead of grabbing the TV remote or *Southern Living* magazine.

Let God in Your House!

Am I to have an open house and invite others over? That's a great idea! Start with hospitality and learn more about your spiritual family. Pro-vide a place for people to come and study or for young people to draw closer to God. Use your sheet rock and plumbing as a haven for those who need a refuge. Don't give a thought about crooked wall hangings, clutter, or dishes in the sink, but invite people in. They won't be able to tell anyone later what it looked like, unless it is dipped in gold and has Liberace's candelabras. No one would ever forget that.

Don't keep the doors locked, shutting God and His people out. Be a loving house. Open your arms and love the brethren. Hug your brothers and sisters. Let them know you care. People respond when you are loving and kind like Jesus. What would you rather people do when they see you come into the church building: Run to see you or run away from you, saying, "Duck! Here she comes"?

We must be open to God's plan for us. Be the house that doesn't fight God but adapts to His plan. Be aware of the opportunities God presents to teach a lost and dying world. Be open to developing more talents to do the work He desires.

David, the shepherd king of Israel, had it in his heart to build God's temple. What did David do when God told him no? Did he kick, scream, and build it anyway? Of course not. He did the next best thing. He planned and gathered materials for his son Solomon. I think David would have helped the next king to build the temple, even if he had not been his son. The only thing that David cared about was pleasing God. David showed unconditional love. That's not only generous, but it's also an example of getting oneself out of the way for the higher good.

Girls, let's be the "house" that accepts God's will and adapts to God's plan. Trust me, that is the house that God wants us to be.

Be a House of Prayer!

Can you imagine Jesus getting so angry with the money-changing Jews that He drove them out of the temple? The temple area was teeming with traveling Jews who were being overcharged when changing their money into the proper "temple money" or when purchasing an animal for sacrifice. In this beautiful edifice to God, men were yelling and shouting and bartering, the animals were bleating and twittering, and the crooks were worshiping gold and silver while robbing their fellowmen. They surrounded the entrance to the main part of the temple. What a noisy scene of chaos greeted those who had arrived for Passover or those who simply wanted to go inside the temple to pray.

All of this infuriated Jesus, and He said, "It is written, 'My house shall be called a house of prayer'; but you are making it a robbers' den" (Matthew 21:13).

My sisters, what have we done with our "house of prayer," our heart for prayer? Can Jesus even call us a "house of prayer"? Have we filled our lives with the love of material things? Has our marvelous Father been offered a back seat in our lives?

Be a prayer warrior. If 1 Thessalonians 5:17 tells us to "pray without ceasing," then we need to do just that. If Colossians 4:2 says, "Devote yourselves to prayer," then we need to do that too. Praying constantly keeps us in touch with the Father and builds our faith. Daniel 6:10 informs us that Daniel knelt to pray three times a day and gave thanks. I believe we need to kneel and pray like Daniel did.

I hear some of you saying, "Do I have to kneel, Becky?" The Father does not command us to kneel when we pray, but we see examples in the Bible of this posture for prayer: Daniel, Jesus, Peter, and Paul. Kneeling is humbling. Stop, kneel, and pray during the day. Just think of all we could accomplish every day if we stopped at least three times a day and humbly praised God and poured our hearts out to Him. Better yet, just think what God could accomplish in our lives if we stopped three times a day and praised Him.

I absolutely do not know how I could ever function without God's gift of prayer. What if we could not speak to our Father? You know the "Begging Place" as well as I do. It is there that God meets us, wraps His arms around us, and comforts us. If He did speak to me personally, I think that He would say, "Oh, My child. Let go. Stop worrying so much. I've got this all handled. Don't you know that by now? You just rest. I am here and I am in charge. Let go and let Me."

Accepting God's will for our lives is not always easy. We pray "Thy will be done," but we surely hope God's will goes along with our will. We want things to turn out the way we want them to, don't we? One of the most important things in waiting is to stop looking for our answer and look for God's answer. How can God's will be accomplished if our own will is in the way? One preacher said,

God answers prayer by doing what He knows is best for us, not what we think might be good for us. Can you recall a time when something you prayed for would have been foolish or maybe even disastrous? As time passes, we look back and realize God's will really was better than our own.[18]

Remember to pray for others. James 5:16 says, "Therefore, confess your sins to one another, and pray for one another so that you may be healed. The effective prayer of a righteous man can accomplish much."

Dr. Jim Gardner, a Bible professor, once said in a sermon, "Focus on something other than yourself. Be concerned with spiritual sickness, not self-fulfillment. Be truly unselfish. Find your life by losing it for Christ." Sweet sisters, true happiness comes when we give ourselves away.

Paul urged the Corinthian church, "You also must help us by prayer, so that many will give thanks on our behalf for the blessing granted us through the prayers of many" (2 Corinthians 1:11 ESV).

Paul wrote to the Ephesian church, "Pray at all times in the Spirit, and with this in view, be on the alert with all perseverance and petition for all the saints" (Ephesians 6:18).

Here is a thought-provoking saying about prayer that was on Facebook anonymously.

> When you find yourself in the position to pray for or help someone, be happy and feel blessed, because God is answering that person's prayer through you. So remember, your purpose on earth is not to get lost in the dark, but to be a light to others that they may find their way through you!

God Always Answers Prayers

Always know that God will not always grant our requests and prayers the way we desire, and we must accept that. The Father knows best. Greg Neill once said in a sermon, "God will do what He wants to do—when He wants to do it—without our permission! That is the sovereignty of God."

God . . . answers prayer, some of the ways are:

He may answer it literally.

He may refuse to grant the petition.

He may send something different from what was requested.

He may answer it gradually.

He may answer it after a long delay.

He may answer through natural laws and processes.[19]

Pause and Ponder

How do you relate to the way God answers prayers? Discuss and share a time when God used one of these methods from Coffman's list above in your life.

We cannot fight God and win. He is the absolute Sovereign, ruler over all things, and His will prevails. It is imperative that our attitude be "Lord willing." My sisters, I cannot impress upon you enough how wonderful God is to give us this marvelous gift of prayer. Make a room in your mind to be your "war room."

Evening, and morning, and at noon, will I pray, and cry aloud: and he shall hear my voice" (Psalm 55:17 KJV). . . . Prayer is man reaching for the heart of God. It is an acknowledgment of human frailty. It is a declaration of man's inability to cope with life on his own. Prayer is man's mind in a state of awe, reverence, and praise at the sovereignty and majesty of God. It is faith accessing grace and pleading for its blessings. It is love honoring God as the object of its profound affection.[20]

Remember that our entire world revolves around Jesus. Our house is built upon Him, and He is our rock. We are to imitate Him and His sacrificial love so that people can see the family resemblance we share with Jesus. Let's ask ourselves, "Do I look like Jesus? What can I do to help someone else?"

Paul wrote, "Be imitators of me, just as I also am of Christ" (1 Corinthians 11:1). Can we make that claim too?

Pause and Ponder

Brainstorm right now and write down five good works that you can do for the Lord.

Find the Time to Give Yourself Away

Living for God and giving yourself to good works make life worth living. This is the Christian's life, or it should be.

An interesting passage in the New Testament is one that quotes Jesus but is not found in the Gospel accounts. In Acts 20:35 Paul said, "In everything I showed you that by working hard in this manner you must help the weak and remember the words of the Lord Jesus, that He Himself said, 'It is more blessed to give than to receive.'" Perhaps Jesus said these words to Paul himself.

Nothing feels better than doing a good deed for someone else. When you take food to a family or sit at a funeral home comforting the grieved, when you pray with a woman who needs help desperately, or when you mow the church's lawn or help tidy the auditorium, you are giving yourself away. And that is what we all are called to do.

At the deaths of each of my parents, the church in Newnan, Georgia, was so kind in surrounding us with constant love and food. The women graciously came to my parents' home each time and provided a wonderful meal before we left for the funeral. I remember thinking to myself, "Becky, from this day on, you must help others who need food when a loved one has passed. Do this for them because now you understand the comfort it provides." If there is a funeral list at your congregation, sign up to help with serving the grieving family and cleaning up, if you can. Sign up to bring food to the church building for the family, or however you gather the funeral food. These are tasks we women know how to do. Please don't be the selfish woman who says, "Oh, let someone else do it. I just don't have the time."

When I help feed a family, I tell myself that I am doing what Jesus would do. I also know what it means to the daughter or the widow who is sitting there, still in shock, now without her loved one. This is my gift to her because I have experienced these circumstances. I know how a broken heart feels.

Kevin Kruse once said, "Life isn't about getting and having. It's about giving and being." So true.

Whom Do You Serve?

I hope and pray that my thoughts from God's Word are reaching your heart. God has given us a mind; what will we do with it? Will we fill it with Him or will we fill it with Satan and the world? I have known wonderful people who chose the pleasures of the world over God. We must realize that if we are not thinking and doing godly actions, then we have already made a choice. Look at it for what it is. We cannot serve God and mammon, and we cannot serve two masters (Matthew 6:24).

God shall have the last say. That is a given. "For the Son of Man is going to come in the glory of His Father with His angels, and will then repay every man according to his deeds" (Matthew 16:27).

God lovingly challenges us to throw everything aside that would turn our hearts away from Him and seek Him. At the same time our Father tells us how to find Him and build a relationship with Him. God is fair. He warns us of the consequences of disobedience and the eternity that follows this life. But He never forces us to love Him, obey Him, or serve Him. That is up to us.

Pause and Ponder

Look up the following passages of His love and assurance: Jeremiah 29:11–13 and Hebrews 13:5–6. What phrases encourage you to seek the precious moments?

How do you know that God is in your corner? Write the sentence that assures you of God's permanence.

The life we have chosen to live is not a game of hide and seek. I believe that God beckons to us across the pages of the Bible, "Find me. I am in plain sight."

The House Now

I may be a slow learner, but I know that when a Christian woman chooses to build her house on the Lord and chooses to be the house with precious godly treasures in the chambers of her mind, then she is living the life God has meant for her to live. She has found herself. She has found the time to walk with God and to be what God wants her to be. Her home is righteous, and God the Father is the Supreme Guest who rules, leads, blesses, and comforts her house.

Lord, give me a vision—of this world's haunting needs.
Why, Lord, must I be burdened with mundane tasks like these?

Lord, give me a vision—of mountains high to climb.
Me—take a pie across the street? No, Lord, You know I
 haven't the time.

Lord, give me a vision—to a closer walk with Thee.
Take who to church? That's quite a drive and You know that
 gasoline is not free!

Lord, give me a vision—so I'll more Christlike be.
And when You have some glorious task, use me—Oh,
 Lord, use me!

—Unknown

MOMENTS IN PRAYER

Oh Lord, help me to find the time to fill my rooms with You. Thank You for all the material and spiritual blessings You so graciously provide for me and my family. You are the epitome of love, and I love You. Please forgive me of my sins and stand with me in the stormy and calm times of my life. I need You so. In Jesus' name, Amen.

 ## Moments in Song

"Make Me a Servant" and "Where Could I Go but to the Lord?"

KEEP SEEKING

1. Name some things we should wisely put in the rooms of our house.
2. What are some of the benefits of being God's child?
3. What works are difficult for you as a Christian?
4. What works are easy for you?

 ## Timely Quotes

"The best gift that you can give anyone is to pray for them."
—Charles Hodge

"I've learned that you shouldn't go through life with a catcher's mitt on both hands; you need to be able to throw something back."

—Maya Angelou

"Just as prayer is our heart crying out to God, His Word, the Bible, is God's heart crying out to us."

—Jeff Jenkins

Satan's Convention

Satan called a worldwide convention. In his opening address to his evil angels, he said, "We can't keep the Christians from going to church. We can't keep them from reading their Bibles and knowing the truth. We can't even keep them from forming an intimate abiding relationship experience in Christ. But if they gain that connection with Jesus, our power over them is broken. So let them go to their churches. Let them have their conservative lifestyles, but steal their time so they can't gain that relationship with Jesus Christ. This is what I want you to do, angels. Distract them from gaining hold of their Savior and maintaining that vital connection throughout their day."

"How shall we do this?" shouted his angels.

"Keep them busy in the non-essentials of life and invent innumerable schemes to occupy their minds," he answered. "Tempt them to spend, spend, spend, and borrow, borrow, borrow. Persuade the wives to go to work for long hours and the husbands to work six or seven days each week, ten to twelve hours a day, so they can afford their empty lifestyles.

"Keep them from spending time with their children. As their family fragments, soon their home will offer no escape from the pressures of work. Entice them to play the radio or CD player whenever they drive. Keep the TV, VCR, DVD, CDs, iPods, and PCs going constantly in their home and see to it that every store and restaurant in the world plays non-biblical music constantly. This will jam their minds and break that union with Christ.

"Fill the coffee tables with magazines and news-papers. Pound their minds with the news twenty-four hours a day. Invade their driving moments with billboards. Flood their mailboxes with junk mail, mail order catalogs, sweepstakes, and every kind of newsletter and promotional offering free products, services, and false hopes. Keep skinny, beautiful models on the magazines so that the husbands will believe that external beauty is what's important, and they'll become dissatisfied with their wives. Ha! That will fragment those families quickly!

"Even in their recreation, let them be excessive. Have them return from their recreation exhausted, disquieted, and unprepared for the coming week. Don't let them go out in nature to reflect on God's wonders. Send them to amusement parks, sporting events, concerts, and movies instead. Keep them busy, busy, busy! Keep them so exhausted that they cannot let their minds dwell on spiritual things, let alone stay awake during worship. And when they meet for spiritual fellowship, involve them in gossip and small talk so that they leave with troubled consciences and unsettled emotions."

It was quite a convention. The evil angels went eagerly to their assignments causing Christians everywhere to get more busy and more rushed, going here and there.

—Unknown Author[21]

CHAPTER 7

Time to Clean That House!

"Clean the house? Are you serious, Ol' Beck?"

"Yes, little chicken, I am."

"But you don't understand. I hate to clean house!"

"So, do I. You are not alone. Trust me, you will be glad you did."

Girls, I cannot let go of this "house" theme running in my head. Let's develop it just a bit more and consider a few more ideas.

A Reason to Clean

Jesus often taught in parables. Simply defined a parable is "an earthly story with a heavenly meaning." Jesus taught in a manner that related to His audience. Just think of the subjects with which the multitudes would identify: a lost sheep, a farmer sowing seed, a dragnet being pulled up from a lake, a bridal party waiting for the bridegroom.

Personally, I love it when Jesus talks about a woman, or helps a woman, or teaches lessons involving a woman. I want to especially know how the words of the Savior apply to me as a woman. In Luke 15 we find three accounts of something or someone being "lost"—a sheep, a coin, and a son. My mom has written, "A parable with three windows," under the chapter's heading in her Bible. Let's focus in on the middle window, the woman with a lost coin.

SEEK THE PRECIOUS MOMENTS

Or what woman, if she has ten silver coins and loses one coin, does not light a lamp and sweep the house and search carefully until she finds it? When she has found it, she calls together her friends and neighbors, saying, "Rejoice with me, for I have found the coin which I had lost!" In the same way, I tell you, there is joy in the presence of the angels of God over one sinner who repents (Luke 15:8–10).

This parable concerns itself with a woman who has lost something very valuable: money. She lights a lamp, sweeps her house, and searches until the coin is found. Then she calls her neighbors to rejoice with her. What meanings does this marvelous parable hold for us?

Many believe it depicts the woman as being the church and the coin is a lost member or a sinner who needs to hear the gospel. The lamp that lights up the entire house—the church—is the word of God which sheds light on the entire world. Now being able to see, the church uses its broom and sweeps out the sin and cleans away the dirt, searching for the one who is lost. The search is not given up until the lost member is found or is converted. Then everyone is called in to rejoice, and there is great rejoicing.

Coffman summarized it this way.

The woman—the church throughout all the ages
The lost coin—the "dropout" from church
The lighted lamp—the word of God
The broom—the church's concern for true virtues and morality
The diligent search—the church's urgent activity to save souls
The rejoicing—the joy in heaven over one who is saved[22]

Wayne Jackson gives depth to understanding the parable:

Near Eastern women highly prized silver coins, sometimes handed down for generations. To lose one was a catastrophe. The common home was small and frequently without windows. Lighting a lamp might be required even in the daytime. Like the sheep, the lost coin represents a lost person. While lost, the coin is of no value to its owner; the lost person cannot be used in God's service. When the coin was found after much searching (evangelism is not easy), there was much rejoicing . . . angels have an interest in the spiritual condition of Christians.[23]

Some feel that the coin is a drachma, a day's wages, which would have been the money provided to sustain life for a woman and her family. In our monetary standard, a drachma would be worth approximately a dollar and twenty cents.

I have also heard the explanation that this lost coin could have been worn around her forehead, representing her dowry—what her husband paid for her. We women can certainly identify with the woman's treasuring the coin that was lost, just as we love our wedding rings, representing the love we share with our husbands.

The Lost Ring

I can personally relate to this parable. I once lost my wedding ring. That was a horrible disaster. I searched like I had never searched before, but the ring was gone. I looked high and low, even in dark corners, but I never found it. To this day, I miss it because my husband put that ring on my finger on our wedding day, and it was my fault that I lost it. I understand this woman's exasperating search.

> The longer a piece of money is lost, the less probability there is of its being again found; as it may not only lose its color, and not be easily observed, but will continue to be more and more covered with dust and dirt: or its value may be vastly lessened by being so trampled on that a part of the substance, together with the image and superscription, may be worn off. So the sinner sinks deeper and deeper into the impurities of sin, loses even his character among men, and gets the image and superscription of his Maker defaced from his heart. He who wishes to find the image of God, which he has lost by sin, must attend to that word which will be a lantern to his steps, and receive that Spirit which is a light to the soul, to convince of sin, righteousness, and judgment. He must sweep the house—put away the evil of his doings; and seek diligently—use every means of

grace, and cry incessantly to God, till he restore to him the light of his countenance.[24]

Pause and Ponder

Read Ephesians 2:10. Underline the word *workmanship.* Then write "handiwork" in the margin. How do you feel about handiwork you create? Why is a soul, God's handiwork, precious to Him?

Jesus Cleaned House!

All four Gospel accounts record that even Jesus had to clean house. He made a scourge whip, overturned tables, and with righteous indignation drove the money changers out of the temple. What was wrong with the moneychangers being in the Lord's house? Surely Jesus understood that travelers would not have the right currency, animals, or birds to offer for their sacrifices. But it was more than that. Jesus had every right to be furious!

These vendors were not in the merciful business of helping their brothers from other cities. They were in the business of helping themselves, scalping their own family tribes for coins and sacrifices. To make matters even more sinister, they had moved their tables into the temple area where these practices were forbidden. Never could the Son of God allow such unholiness in the house of God.

> These animals and birds were required offerings in the Jewish sacrifices, but the worshipers were required to purchase them from the temple functionaries and were not allowed to bring their own; and even in circumstances where the worshiper might have been permitted to bring his own offering, the element of convenience naturally turned all to the supply provided by the temple. Also, the only money that could be used in such purchases was the coinage or currency controlled by the temple. The denarius and other coins were prohibited, for example, as bearing Caesar's image. Thus, with

the temple concessionaires having the only supply of animals and the only supply of money by which they could have been purchased, the suffering people were gouged unmercifully. No wonder Jesus denounced that crowd of cheaters as "thieves and robbers." It was particularly an act of aggravation that the money-changers had actually moved into the sacred area of the temple itself.[25]

Clean, Search, Expose, Restore

My friends, we are in the "cleaning, searching, and lighting business." Jesus said He was "the way, the truth, the life," and "the light" (John 14:6; 8:12). He is our standard for helping the lost to find their way home.

We are searching for those who have never obeyed the gospel. We are lighting the lamp of the Bible and teaching a lost and dying world. We are also in the restoration business. Sometimes Christians fall away from the faith, and we are to blame. Perhaps we didn't help them enough or love them enough or teach them enough. Perhaps they are babes in Christ, and we don't nourish them and help them grow. What do we do now? We are on a "search and rescue" mission. We go after them and lovingly light the way with the Word, the Bible.

That is our mission. The parable of the lost sheep, told by Jesus just before that of the lost coin, illustrates the value of a lost soul. The shepherd left the saved sheep and went in search of the lost sheep. He searched and searched until he found the lost sheep. When he found it, he laid it on his shoulders and rejoiced.

Jesus made sure that each parable in Luke 15 had a happy ending with the lost being found. Don't we love the rejoicing part—the shepherd (Jesus), the friends and neighbors (the angels)? Of course we do. When we restore a brother or sister, or when we are able to teach someone and they become a Christian, what rejoicing there is! Why is there so much joy? Because one sinner has come home. I frequently see this quote by Don Lessin, "What a privilege we have been given by God to be able to spend our lives giving His love away." Giving His love away is why we are here. It is an honor to show the love of God, share that love, and teach that love daily.

Sometimes I, like the woman in the parable, must stop, light the lamp, and sweep my house. I must clean it up and throw out any error. I need to inspect every corner and look high and low to evict any wrong. I must make sure that my slate is clean, and that nothing stands between the Lord and me. I need to ask for forgiveness and get my life right with God. If not, how can I help someone who has fallen away or needs to hear the truth? Hebrews 4:12 tells us that God's Word is sharper than any two-edged sword. It cuts us, changes us, and shows us how to shape up and live for Him.

The Bible is the standard by which we compare any religion or doctrines, and it is the supreme authority to show us how to walk with the Lord, to live purely and holy.

When I light the lamp in my house, that light—the Word of God—exposes error that might creep inside. It is up to me to toss it out.

Pause and Ponder

Look up these passages on darkness and light: Matthew 5:14–15; John 3:19–21; 2 Corinthians 4:4; Ephesians 1:18

Sometimes the church allows error to creep under her door. What do we do then? We light the lamp of His instructing Word, use the broom to sweep out the error, and get right with God. That is not always easy, for some Christians adopt error and then balk when the church takes a stand for right.

The world has captured the hearts of many in the church. They think, act, talk, dress, and recreate like those who claim no religion. They desire a comfort zone in the church and the world. They want enough association with God to soothe the conscience and sufficient coalition with the world to gratify the flesh. They want God without sacrifice and the world without guilt. There are members of the church who are friends of the world and enemies of God (James 4:4), and they lack the ability to discern it.[26]

Sin creeps into our lives effortlessly, and we become desensitized to it. We are no longer shocked by vulgarity, sex jokes, and pornography the media attempt to put before our eyes. The department store ads arrive in our mailbox, full of lingerie models in skimpy attire, and we excuse it by saying, "Oh, that is just the world we live in."

We need to turn off the TV with its filthy agenda, and turn on good music—or watch good DVDs. It is therapeutic to turn off the noise or read the Bible and good material that is pure. When the devil is at the door, don't open that door! Instead, we must make the effort to let our minds dwell on good things (Philippians 4:8). Living for God certainly means that Satan is absolutely not welcome in our house.

Give the Devil the Boot

When I get distracted, Satan turns my attention away from Jesus and tempts me to fill my house with worldly materialistic pleasures. Remember, the very last thing Satan wants is for us to share the gospel, but first, Satan must get us. Is he pleased when we are so busy that we don't have time to teach, encourage, or rescue a lost soul? Satan cleverly whispers, "Your plate is already too full. You're much too busy right now."

My mom shared the following poem with me, and I have written it in the back of my Bible. I hope you do the same.

A Rule to Govern My Life

Anything that dims my vision of Christ
Or takes away my taste for Bible study
Or cramps my prayer life
Or makes Christian work difficult
Is wrong for me.

I must, as a Christian,
Turn away from it.

—John Wilbur Chapman[27]

What can I do to prevent falling for Satan's ploys? I must be on my toes and aware of his luring ways. Peter warned the church to be aware of the devil when he wrote, "Be of sober spirit, be on the alert. Your adversary, the devil, prowls around like a roaring lion, seeking someone to devour" (1 Peter 5:8).

I also need to be dressed properly with my armor on. I never get tired of reading Paul's letter to the church at Ephesus, describing the Christian's armor that defeats Satan:

> Finally, be strong in the Lord and in the strength of His might. Put on the full armor of God, so that you will be able to stand firm against the schemes of the devil. For our struggle is not against flesh and blood, but against the rulers, against the powers, against the world forces of this darkness, against the spiritual forces of wickedness in the heavenly places. Therefore, take up the full armor of God, so that you will be able to resist in the evil day, and having done everything, to stand firm (Ephesians 6:13–17).

Pause and Ponder

Research the meaning of "forces of this darkness" in the above text. Copy the full armor of God from Ephesians 6:14–17. Is there a piece of armor you need more than others? Circle it.

Clean Your Mind

Above all I must seek the truth and only the truth. We have a higher purpose than reading novels or repeating tales of the past, even though some of these are entertaining. We are to seek godliness for now and always.

But have nothing to do with worldly fables fit only for old women. On the other hand, discipline yourself for the purpose of godliness; for bodily discipline is only of little profit, but godliness is profitable for all things, since it holds promise for the present life and also for the life to come (1 Timothy 4:7–8).

Like David, I too must "set no worthless thing before my eyes" (Psalm 101:3). I must put things into my house that will help me get to heaven. I must enrich my mind, heart, and faith with godly things that will help me on my journey with the Lord. Paul put it beautifully:

> Finally, brethren, whatever is true, whatever is honorable, whatever is right, whatever is pure, whatever is lovely, whatever is of good repute, if there is any excellence and if anything worthy of praise, dwell on these things (Philippians 4:8).

Coffman's Commentary says this about verse 8: "Thinking of such things will lead to speaking of them, thus contributing to the joy and unity of Christian fellowship. . . . Let such things shape your attitudes."[28]

Clean Up the Mess

It is extremely important, my sisters, that we all do spring, summer, fall, and winter housecleaning—not a little, but a lot. Let's light the lamp of God's Word and rid ourselves of whatever stands between us and God. We have to get right with God. Nothing is more important. When we decide to get back on the right track, our brothers, sisters, and angels rejoice with us because they too know sin and Satan's influence.

Jim Sheerer wrote, "Whenever a person rejects God and the will of God, he will make a mess of his life. . . . Everyone who sins suffers the consequences of sin."[29] So true.

Guard your precious spirit, given by God. One of these days, your life on this planet will be over, and your spirit will return to God who gave it.

> Then the dust will return to the earth as it was, and the spirit will return to God who gave it (Ecclesiastes 12:7).

And Jesus, crying out with a loud voice, said, "Father, into Thy hands I commit my spirit" (Luke 23:46).

The way we live here will determine our destiny—heaven or hell. Where will our souls go?

We have lived long enough to personally know brothers and sisters who loved the Lord and seemed to be on the right path. But unfortunately, they fell away from the Lord. In spite of restoration efforts, they never came back. Satan surely gloats when he is able to pull any Christian away from God's family. Always remember to pray for those who have fallen away. Don't give up on them. Pray for time for them to come to their senses and repent.

Satan works hard in all of our lives—in all of our houses. He is bent on destruction, but the Lord is bent on construction. Keep on praying. We are all in the family of God, and together we love and help one another.

God is better than any "Home Depot" or *Fixer Upper* when it comes to helping us change and reconstruct our lives into the blueprint He has in mind for us.

Please stop and write 1 John 4:4 on your heart. Underline it in your Bible and memorize it: "You are from God, little children, and have overcome them; because greater is He who is in you than he who is in the world." Here is God's assurance that He is in us and is greater and more powerful than Satan will ever be. It is God who is our Father, not Satan. That is one of my favorite comfort scriptures.

He Learned Obedience

He obeyed God and that proved His love,
And now He lives with the Father above.
His words are not grievous;
His burden is light.
They bring peace and comfort
Through day and through night.

It's not long 'til we join Him,
So no matter the cost,
Keep me close to Jesus,
And not lost with the lost.

—Lea Fowler, used by permission

MOMENTS IN PRAYER

Oh Lord, You are so kind and so good to me. Thank You for all the blessings You give me and for answering my prayers. Please help me to find the time to clean my house from roof to foundation, and please, Lord, help me to keep it clean. I love You with all my heart. Please bless the church. In Jesus' name, Amen.

Moments in Song

"I Am a Sheep and the Lord Is My Shepherd" and "Trust and Obey"

KEEP SEEKING

1. Name some ways Satan easily distracts you and your family.
2. How important in the parable of the lost coin is lighting the lamp?
3. What is that lamp?

Timely Quotes

"Yesterday I was clever, so I wanted to change the world.
Today I am wise, so I am changing myself."

—Rumi

"When growth stops, decay begins!"

—Unknown

"We are not given a good life or a bad life. We are given a life. It is up to us to make it good or bad."

—Ward Foley

Let It Begin Today

I love rain; sweet, sweet rain. It pours down from heaven and answers many prayers here in Texas. When I lived in Georgia, I took rain for granted. But in Texas, we have a "whole 'nother" appreciation for it. Rain is a huge deal here. Let me tell you about a certain touching rain event.

It was a Saturday. The skies opened up, and rain came to Waco—all day and all night long. It was certainly a temptation to stay inside, but this Saturday was different. Jeff and I decided to visit two church friends, one in a rehabilitation center, and one in an assisted living facility. We visited ninety-two-year-old Blanche, who had the sweetest apartment you ever did see. We stayed more than an hour, making sure she received a chocolate treat. The rain was pouring when we arrived, and it was pouring when we left.

Our next stop was to see Patsy, an older Christian sister who had been in and out of rehab because of intestinal surgery. Patsy always had a smile on her face, and we were anxious to see her and give her a little fancy tote filled with snacks and candy. But when we got to Patsy's room, the bed was empty and made. We learned that she had gone home the day before.

We then got into the elevator with another family—a young family. The father was pushing his wife in a wheelchair. She was a patient at the rehab center. On her lap were two precious children, loving the free ride. The mother must have had a stroke, because it was difficult for her to speak or move, but we tried to chat. I decided to give her the tote of snacks and candy, and her children were delighted about that. Her little girl held the tote very tightly. We came to the ground floor, and all of us got off the elevator.

Now remember, it was pouring rain. But this woman wanted her husband to push her to the very edge of the opened front door so that she could see and feel it. She didn't care if her feet got wet. She didn't care if she got wet. She just wanted to get as close as possible to the open air and rain.

My heart hurt for her, for her husband, and for her children. She was much too young for this experience, but she was happy, happy to be with her family and happy to see the rain. We all said goodbye, and Jeff and I were off into the elements.

I can still see that little family in my mind, but it is the woman that makes me pause. In the midst of her struggles, which were huge, she could smile and be thankful. This lovely woman, with her children on her lap and her husband by her side, was happy, even though trapped in a wheelchair. She had every reason not to smile. But she smiled. She had every reason to feel sorry for herself. But she was at peace.

I hope I don't forget her. None of us knows what tomorrow will bring. Our lives can change drastically. The older we get, the more we realize how subject to change we are. Anything is possible. All the more reason for us to be on our toes examining our lives and thanking God that we are alive. Tomorrow may bring a wheelchair for us.

The psalmist was inspired to write: "This is the day which the Lord has made; let us rejoice and be glad in it" (Psalm 118:24). How important it is to treasure the day and make the most of our opportunities. Give God the glory for all things. May we be committed to living a life full of loving and serving others like Jesus did. Why can't we be like Jesus?

I am challenging us to start early in our efforts to be thankful for our blessings. Let us put aside the daily stresses that wear us down and start counting our many blessings. Before our feet touch the floor in the morning, let's begin by thanking God for something. Aren't you thankful for a good bed and pillow? I surely am.

Paul was inspired to challenge the church at Thessalonica to live gratefully, saying, "In everything give thanks; for this is God's will for you in Christ Jesus" (1 Thessalonians 5:18).

In everything, give thanks. And let's be a blessing wherever we go. Life on this planet is short, so let's make every day count. Enjoy the sun and treasure the rain. Remember, God is good all the time.

Becky Blackmon

CHAPTER 8

Time to Take Care of You!

I can recall my mom saying on many occasions as we parted, "Becky, take care of yourself. Remember, you cannot be replaced." My sweet sisters, please heed that warning too. From this older woman to you younger women, please listen: Find time for you. Get your rest when you can. Take care of your health; take your vitamins. Escape to the park and walk the track. Pray as you walk. Be a Hannah—pour out your heart to God.

Exercise, swim, or run if you can. Take the stairs instead of the elevator. Park in the outer parking lot at Walmart and count your steps from your car to the entrance. Dr. Oz says that we need to take ten thousand steps a day.

As a jolly older woman once told me, "My body is a vessel for God, and I must be a good steward of it. When I get to heaven, I am going to trade it in for the Lamborghini vessel God has prepared for me." Being a good steward is taking care of your house. Your body needs lots of exercise and oxygen. No one will take better care of your body than you, so listen to it and heed its warning signals and needs. Getting your exercise makes you feel good and increases confidence levels.

"Know thyself," Socrates once said.

"Know thyself or at least keep renewing the acquaintance," Robert Breault has said.

If you are on vacation at the beach, arise before sunrise, walk along the beach, and meditate on God's love and handiwork. On a mountain trip? Put your feet in a cold mountain spring, look at the tall trees and blue sky, and ponder the magnificence of God the Creator. Get your rest and take vacations that offer opportunities for relaxation, not the constant go, go, go!

Pause and Ponder

Read Ecclesiastes 2:24; 3:13; 5:18–20; 8:15; 9:9. Search for and circle the common phrase similar to "the gift of God."

Just Talkin' to the Lord

We are surrounded by young and old addicted to cell phones and iPads. Some cannot even walk down the street without being glued to their phones, never looking where they are going.

Put away the electronics, remove any earbuds, and talk to the Lord. Pray as you walk or exercise. I love to swim, and my favorite song to swim by is "We Praise Thee, O God!" Find the joy in being alone with God. Look at the world with which He has surrounded you, and thank Him for the blessings of your area. Take note of birds, trees, skies, and clouds. Learn to enjoy the peace and quiet of natural settings: the mountains, the ocean, and the desert. God has prepared a veritable feast for the eyes as we gaze at the world around us. How magnificent is our Maker!

Pray for the people you love and don't love. As you walk around the block, pray for the new converts, the new babies at your congregation, and the visitors that are searching for a church home. Pray to be that extension cord that plugs a sinner into Jesus. Pray to have courage to tell others about the gospel. Pray, pray, pray!

Be happy in your own skin. Oscar Wilde once said, "Be yourself. Everyone else is already taken." Isn't that good? Don't be something you're not. Janis Joplin once said, "Don't compromise yourself. You are all you've got."

Mom used to tell me when I was growing up: "To thine own self be true, Beck." When we are young, we want to be like the in crowd: dress the same way; talk the same way; look the same way. But God calls us to be different.

> But you are a chosen race, a royal priesthood, a holy nation, a people for God's own possession, so that you may proclaim the excellencies of Him who has called you out of darkness into His marvelous light (1 Peter 2:9).

You are a holy nation. Called out. Called out of what? The world. We are in the world but not of the world. Be holy in the way you dress—not holey!

Laugh, Laugh, and Laugh Some More

Have you noticed that signs are the in thing now? Long signs, short signs, dark signs, and white signs, all with a message to be displayed in our homes. I love them, particularly those with Scriptures written on them.

The one I see the most is "Live, Laugh, and Love." Not a bad idea. We must live this life, so why not laugh and love and make it wonderful? I like to focus on the laughter because having a sense of humor makes life livable. I love what Erma Bombeck said: "If you can't make it better, you can laugh at it." And Ethel Barrymore quipped, "You grow up the day you have your first real laugh at yourself."

Skip the Drama!

Learn to laugh at yourself and be a good sport. There is nothing more disgusting than being with a girl in a group that sulks and selfishly wants her way and all the attention—a real drama queen. Evidently this is the way she was raised, and her mama put up with it instead of handling it. What irks us when a sulky Sue is around is that the rest of us have to deal with her drama. If I'd ever tried that sulky behavior while growing up, my mom would have immediately inflicted an attitude adjustment with her favorite hairbrush. She never allowed us to act like spoiled brats. She quickly dealt with unacceptable behavior.

Someone once said, "We should be so busy loving God, loving others, and loving our lives that we have no time for regrets, worries, fears, or drama." Now that's a saying we need to put into practice.

God has given us so many fabulous proverbs to show us the importance of having a positive spirit. Look at these passages.

- "A joyful heart makes a cheerful face, but when the heart is sad, the spirit is broken" (Proverbs 15:13).

- "All the days of the afflicted are bad, but a cheerful heart has a continual feast" (Proverbs 15:15).

- "A joyful heart is good medicine, but a broken spirit dries up the bones" (Proverbs 17:22).

Precious Moments of Prayer

Other than His Son, I believe that the most wonderful gift God has given us in all His mercy and kindness is the gift of prayer. Talking with God, communicating with Him, and being able to tell Him everything on our hearts are great blessings known only to His children. To be able to come into the Lord's throne room confidently and lay everything at His feet brings great peace. Having Jesus to intercede on our behalf assures us of help in time of need.

> Therefore, since we have a great high priest who has passed through the heavens, Jesus the Son of God, let us hold fast our confession. For we do not have a high priest who cannot sympathize with our weaknesses, but One who has been tempted in all things as we are, yet without sin. Therefore let us draw near with confidence to the throne of grace, so that we may receive mercy and find grace to help in time of need (Hebrews 4:14–16).

We pray because we know God can fix whatever is wrong in our lives. We pray because we have faith that God knows what is best for us. We pray because we need to talk to our Father. C. S. Lewis said, "I pray because I can't help myself. I pray because I'm helpless. I pray because the need flows out of me all the time—waking and sleeping. It doesn't change God. It changes me."

Just as Jesus had to escape to quiet places and talk to His Father, so do we. Praying clears our heads and hearts. It draws us closer to the one who made us and loves us unconditionally. Talking to the Father increases the relationship we have with one another.

- Matthew 14:23—"After He had sent the crowds away, He went up on the mountain by Himself to pray; and when it was evening, He was there alone."

- Luke 5:16—"But Jesus Himself would often slip away to the wilderness and pray."

- Luke 6:12—"It was at this time that He went off to the mountain to pray, and He spent the whole night in prayer to God."

Jesus had to reconnect with His Father. Are we any different? Are we able to endure separation from our mighty fortress called God? Even God's Son could not, so how can we? Why do you think Jesus chose quiet places to pray? Luke records that it was Jesus' habit to go to the Mount of Olives. Why there? The Garden of Gethsemane is there, a peaceful respite away from Jerusalem's constant noise and voices. Here Jesus could pray and think. We certainly can understand that.

Pause and Ponder

Read Luke 22:39 in your Bible. What is your habit or custom for prayer? Why is it important to establish a routine pattern for praying? What can you do to improve your prayer life and slow down?

Time of Exhaustion

When I read of Jesus' falling asleep on a boat, I can feel His exhaustion. It was impossible for Him to slow down because time was of essence. There was so much for Jesus to do, but there was little time to accomplish it.

> Think of the time that Jesus got into a boat and promptly fell asleep (Mark 4:36–39). Did He fall asleep due to the sheer exhaustion of His mission? Haven't we experienced that same kind of exhaustion when we collapse on our sofa after a horrid day? Retreating to the mountains to talk to His Father was Jesus' lifeline. Escaping on a fishing boat was therapy. These retreats helped Him to stay the course.[30]

Girls, it is easier to talk to the Lord when our surroundings are tranquil and calm. Don't get me wrong, we certainly can call on the name of the Lord on a busy street or surrounded by a cacophony of noisy disturbances. But I have found that it is during the quiet moments of the day that I can mentally escape and talk to my Father in heaven. Do not be afraid to reach over and turn that television or CD player off. Find the time for peace and quiet and the Lord every day, and your life will be better and blessed.

Time for the Body

You'll probably read this section and say, "Well, ol' Beck went to meddling." I hate to say this because we girls are so conscious of weight and appearance. But let me go out on a limb and say it: Girls, we have to take care of our bodies, and that includes watching our weight. Now please hear me on this: I am preaching to myself here. I need to be better about my diet and exercise—and I am definitely *not* a size two!

At least one sister must be saying to herself, "Yeah, I watch my weight—watch it go right up the scale!" Or another says, "I am on the seafood diet. When I see food, I eat it!" I know what you mean. I enjoy eating food, preparing food, and shopping for food. I just like food! (Mashed potatoes and gravy are my favorites.) I have a closet full of clothes of all sizes. And I have clothes from other decades too, because they just might come back in style.

Women need women; that is a given. How thankful I am for the women God has sent into my life. I simply don't know if I could live without them. The Scriptures tell us to help one another, love one another, and bear one another's burden. Therefore, sweet sisters, I'll share something that has opened my eyes. Remember, I am a slow learner, and you may already have grasped the concept I want to share.

My good friend, Sharon Gardner, a wonderful preacher's wife in Vermont, really enlightened me on this topic of our bodies—our physical houses. She made me stop and think seriously and soberly about the importance of eating right and tending carefully to my physical body.

Here is what Sharon has to say:

This battle I fight with my fleshly body is not a fight against fat or diseases. It is a fight against Satan. It is a spiritual fight because Satan doesn't want me to be all that I can be as a Christian. Satan wants to see me discouraged, unhealthy, and unable to physically carry out all the work the Lord has for me to do.

As a Christian, I am in a spiritual battle, described in Ephesians 6. And my battle against unhealthy eating is part of my spiritual battle. Satan doesn't want me to succeed in being able to physically and mentally carry out my work for God. He wants me to fail.

I only have this one physical body to house the spirit God gave me. My body is a temple for His spirit to call "home" while I fight the "schemes of the devil" mentioned in Ephesians 6:11. If this body fails because of the abuse I give it, then I am helping Satan defeat me.

This physical body only has a short time on this earth. God may choose to let that time end sooner than I think, by circumstances beyond my control. But I do control how I treat my body. Will I have the physical health to do all He has in mind? I must make myself ready for His will.

Let's seek precious moments to care for our bodies. How can God use us if we are sick, overweight, and unable to get around? How can we go, teach the lost, or study the Bible with someone when we ourselves cannot move? So Satan loves to glorify food. He knows that if we give precedence to food, God cannot rule us. I truly had never thought of Satan's doing that until I listened to Sharon. How sad it would be to be unable to work the plan God has in mind for us (Jeremiah 29:11–13).

My sweet sisters, let me urge you to get your rest. Put your feet up for a while. Take a nap. As you grow older, you will not have the energy you once did and you will need more rest. That is normal. I surely don't like it, but it's normal. Take care of your temple. I think J. Meyer was right when she said, "I believe that the greatest gift you can give your family and the world is a healthy you."

Learn to Say No

That little two-letter word no is probably one of the hardest for us women to say. We want to help others; we see situations crying out for our attention, and then a PTA meeting is suddenly slotted in the only space available to sit down and collapse.

Girls, learn to say no. You cannot do everything people want or expect you to do. You are not Superwoman, remember? You will never please everyone, and many people do not care about the burdens they put on you. God is the one we must please, so organize your days to please Him. It is wise to eliminate unnecessary appointments and meetings. It frees you up to pray more, study God's word more, and be with your family more. Then perhaps you'll even have time to help someone else. We are no good to the Lord if we are tired and exhausted all the time. Pray about your schedule and ask God for more time to gain your strength.

Nobody loves us as God does. He will take care of us because He loves us, and we are His daughters. The Father, Son, and Holy Spirit are the focus of our lives. We must know them. Let's invest precious moments to work on a meaningful relationship with them.

Jesus whispers across the ages and the pages of the Bible to us and asks one question, "For what does it profit a [woman] to gain the whole world, and lose [her] own soul?" (Mark 8:36).

Feeding Body and Soul

The very first thing we need to do is stop and pray to the Father for guidance and wisdom in being healthy. We must take an honest look at our eating habits—especially our family's eating habits—remove the bad stuff in our life or house, and then diligently rebuild our life and fill our house with God, the right food, and good things.

The Lord knew we would need fantastic passages to help change our lives and make it possible for us to live for Him. Paul's outstanding epistle to the Colossians lists elements we sweep out of our lives. Then he lists replacements to prevent empty places. By the way, when God gives us a list, we need to sit up and pay attention. Take note of the following "take off" list and a "put on" list for our houses. As my sweet sister Sandra from Chattanooga says, "You have to put off before you can put on."

> But now you also, put them all aside: anger, wrath, malice, slander, and abusive speech from your mouth. Do not lie to one another, since you laid aside the old self with its evil practices, and have put on the new self who is being renewed to a true knowledge according to the image of the One who created him (Colossians 3:8–10).

> So, as those who have been chosen of God, holy and beloved, put on a heart of compassion, kindness, humility, gentleness and patience; bearing with one another, and forgiving each other, whoever has a complaint against anyone; just as the Lord forgave you, so also should you. Beyond all these things put on love, which is the perfect bond of unity (Colossians 3:12–14).

Pause and Ponder

Read Colossians 3:1–17 and point out the passages that you instantly relate to. Tell why.

Filling an Empty House

When Jesus lived on earth, the crowds and multitudes continually followed Him from city to city, often demanding a sign. On one occasion, Jesus turned and addressed the crowd who again wanted to see a miracle.

> Now when the unclean spirit goes out of a man, it passes through waterless places seeking rest, and does not find it. Then it says, 'I will return to my house from which I came; and when it comes, it finds it unoccupied, swept, and put in order. Then it goes and takes along with it seven other spirits more wicked than itself, and they go in and live there; and the last state of that man becomes worse than the first. That is the way it will also be with this evil generation (Matthew 12:43–45).

What do you think Jesus was teaching at this moment? He was stressing the importance of filling our lives with good and not evil. To not fill a scrubbed and cleaned life with God will result in a filthy existence.

How important for every Christian to heed these words about an unoccupied house from our Savior. When we become Christians, our sins are forgiven, and our houses are clean. We are ready to walk with the Lord. We want to please Him, and we wear the name Christian proudly. What does the name Christian really mean? It means "Christ like."

The Christian look likes Christ and portrays Christ in behavior, speech, example, dress—the whole package. Our clean dwellings must have something to replace all the former sinful ways and sensual behaviors that once lived in us.

Remember that key proverb we talked about earlier? "By wisdom a house is built, and by understanding it is established; and by knowledge the rooms are filled with all precious and pleasant riches" (Proverbs 24:3–4).

If we do not fill the rooms of our minds with good pieces, spiritual matters, and wholesome friends and activities, then Satan will move right back in, bringing his demon friends, and they will take over. What would God in heaven want us to do with our forgiven life? Jesus left us with the "church's marching orders":

> Go therefore and make disciples of all the nations, baptizing them in the name of the Father and the Son and the Holy Spirit, teaching them to observe all that I commanded you; and lo, I am with you always, even to the end of the age (Matthew 28:19–20).

There are souls to be saved, so we must get into the Word, fill ourselves with knowledge and know-how in order to help the lost find their way home to God. We need to know the plan of salvation and give money to support missionaries. Better yet, be the missionary. Be the right livin', God fearin', gospel preachin', Bible knowin', and Bible totin' Christian machine that can go anywhere, anytime, anyplace to keep some soul from a horrible eternal torment called hell. That is our job. Learn to "speak the truth in love" (Ephesians 4:15) and be a blessing to everyone.

Go on a mission trip and see what goes on in the mission field. Do volunteer work for a congregation that has little money. Be a part of Sojourners—Christian volunteers who travel around the country, paying their own expenses, and helping congregations with repairs, VBS, and other special events. A great gift to give a Christian camp is your time in the kitchen or a teaching role for a camping session.

Girls, I cannot explain the therapeutic benefits of spiritual retreats; they're food for the soul. Some national retreats are held annually for women who want to spend a weekend with their sisters of like faith and grow in the knowledge of the Bible. Be a part of a retreat, or plan a retreat for your congregation so that the women can become closer to God and to one another. Go to another congregation's retreat in another city or state and enjoy being revived.

Pause and Ponder

Comment on at least two ways you can fill your "rooms."

Spare Time Is Precious

Make a conscious effort to use spare time to meditate on the love of God. We have more time than we think to pray and dwell on spiritual thoughts during the day. Paul wrote these instructions: "Finally, brethren, whatever is true, whatever is honorable, whatever is right, whatever is pure, whatever is lovely, whatever is of good repute, if there is any excellence and if anything worthy of praise, dwell on these things" (Philippians 4:8).

Listen to Jane McWhorter:

> Make use of routine tasks. Have you ever thought about how many hours you spend working in the kitchen each week? If you allot fifteen minutes each for breakfast and lunch, and thirty minutes for dinner, the time amounts to seven hours a week—almost a full working day. That amounts to 364 hours a year, the equivalent of nine forty-hour workweeks! If you think that number is unrealistic, cut it in half. Would that be more time in meditation than you are investing now?
>
> You may consider the time spent doing routine tasks as wasted and begrudge it, or you may count it as a blessing. It all depends on your attitude.
>
> After all, cleaning a kitchen is very mechanical. Your hands have performed the task so often they know what to do with very little mental effort. Instead of thinking of the seven hours lost each week, consider the time as a gift—seven hours each week for thinking. As your hands and feet do physical work, let your mind dwell on spiritual concepts. Be vigilant in looking for opportunities to increase your spirituality, along with that of your family.[31]

Jane is right. It is not difficult to perform simple tasks such as mowing the lawn or vacuuming or washing the dishes while letting our minds dwell on godly matters.

Paul urged the Colossian church, "Let the word of Christ richly dwell within you" (Colossians 3:16). Note that the word of Christ is to richly dwell, not poorly dwell. And the only way we can know the Word is to open our Bibles daily and read. When we know what the Bible says, we are stronger and more faithful to God.

What a total waste of a life and a soul—to be converted and then to turn back to Satan's worldliness and a life without God!

> For if, after they have escaped the defilements of the world by the knowledge of the Lord and Savior Jesus Christ, they are again entangled in them and are overcome, the last state has become worse for them than the first. For it would be better for them not to have known the way of righteousness, than having known it, to turn away from the holy commandment handed on to them. It has happened to them according to the true proverb, "A dog returns to its own vomit," and, "A sow, after washing, returns to wallowing in the mire" (2 Peter 2:20–22).

I believe these are some of the saddest verses in the Bible, don't you? God has made sure we get the message here. It is disturbingly graphic. If God has honored us with the blessing of hearing the gospel of Jesus, the privilege of obeying the gospel, the blessing of forgiving all our sins, and the opportunity of going to heaven, and then we return to our evil ways, it would have been better if we had never become a Christian! A dog eating his own vomit and a sow wallowing in the slop are disgusting and sickening. It is more disgusting and sickening to reject God's love and mercy and Christ's sacrifice. It is trampling on Jesus and His life given in our stead. Who would ever want to do that?

Let's read what the Hebrews writer was inspired to say on this matter:

> How much severer punishment do you think he will deserve who has trampled under foot the Son of God, and has regarded as unclean the blood of the covenant by which he was sanctified, and has insulted the Spirit of grace? (Hebrews 10:29).

Don't Let Go!

When I obeyed the gospel of Christ, I made the decision to follow Jesus. There is no higher calling. I poured the foundation of my house, my life, and my world with Him, His words, and His teachings. He is my rock. Why do I follow Jesus? Because He died for me. He gave His all. I cannot stand and gaze at His blood-covered body on an old rugged cross and walk away. No way! If Christ could give His all, then so can I. I can be that living sacrifice mentioned in Romans 12:1. I will lie down on that altar of the Lord and offer myself.

As I sit here and pour out these words, my heart is broken. Why? Because some people whom I have loved through the years once served Jesus. Now they have let Him go. They now live a life described by the Old Testament as doing what is right in their own eyes (Judges 17:6). That is their lifestyle. No God. No Jesus. No Holy Spirit. Just vomit and slop. They have broken their parents' hearts, others' hearts, and my heart and simply walked away.

You probably know what I am talking about. Perhaps you have a broken heart too. What do we do, my sisters? We never give up hope. We never stop praying for them. These prayer times for special friends occur in the wee hours of the morning or late in the evening or as I sit on an airplane, gazing at the clouds and marveling at God's supremacy and majesty. And I wonder in my heart of hearts, "Oh sweet sister of mine, how could you possibly look at the cross and walk away?"

So many times, when I was saying goodbye to Mom, she would look at me and say, "Remember, Becky, you cannot be replaced." So I say to you as you read this book, "Remember, my sweet sister, please take care of yourself. You cannot be replaced."

MOMENTS IN PRAYER

Oh, Lord, we thank You for the body and the life You have given us. Please help us to live a life that pleases You, not disappoints You. Please help us, Lord, to take care of our physical and mental health. Bless us and make us strong for You. Please help us find the time to take care of us. In Jesus' name, Amen.

Moments in Song

"All to Jesus I Surrender" and "My Hope Is Built on Nothing Less"

ℭKEEP SEEKING℈

1. Research the poem "If I Had My Life to Live Over" copyrighted by Erma Bombeck, and read it aloud. Discuss the biblical basis. I found it on this web link: http://www.kalimunro.com/If_I_Had_My_Life_To_Live_Over.html.

2. Do you think your house needs a good housecleaning?

3. Why is it so important to quickly fill our house with God and good things?

❝ Timely Quotes ❞

"One reason we are so harried and hurried is that we make yesterday and tomorrow our business, when all that legitimately concerns us is today. If we really have too much to do, there are some items on the agenda which God did not put there. Let us submit the list to Him and ask Him to indicate which items we must delete. There is always time to do the will of God. If we are too busy to do that, we are too busy."

—Elisabeth Elliot

"Take rest; a field that has rested gives a beautiful crop."

—Ovid

"Your time is limited, so don't waste it living someone else's life."

—Steve Jobs

Tom Fowler,
Russ Fowler,
Lea Fowler,
Judy Fowler Ault,
Becky Fowler Blackmon

Russ Fowler,
Becky Blackmon,
Judy Ault,
Tom Fowler,
Lea Fowler

Mom
and Dad

TIME WITH BECKY

The Memory Porch

My dad built my mom a lovely winterized porch in the last house they occupied. She adored all the shelves covering the walls on which to place her antique dish collections, travel souvenirs, and pictures of relatives and friends. She had two love seats and a long dining table out there too. Everything was decorated in white and blue. When you walked onto the porch, you felt that you either were on the ocean or walking on the beach.

Mom loved to sit on her porch and talk to visitors, strangers, and friends. I remember walking around this porch, gazing at the pictures and asking questions. I loved seeing my younger mom and dad and their relatives. I would see these family pictures on the wall and on her tables around the porch and say, "Who are they, Mom? Who was she? Who was that child?" And she would tell me the history of that relative and what she remembered about them. I did not always take the time to learn or remember each one.

Sometimes Mom bought antique pictures of people she didn't even know, simply because she loved the ornate frames. And yes, there were people in lovely frames who adorned the walls of her home whom none of us knew. Mom bought two particular old-fashioned photographs of a Victorian couple. The woman looked exactly like my mom, only with long hair fashioned into a "Gibson girl" bun. The couple was displayed in lovely tortoise-shell frames and hung very stately in the foyer. For years my husband thought the lady was his mother-in-law's mother. One day we told him the truth. He has never fully recovered.

Since my parents' deaths, I have inherited many of their pictures. I stop now and look at those photographs and think, "Oh, who was that?" Mom did tell me. Was that her uncle who suffered shell shock in WWI, the one who would fall apart at any sudden noise? Was that Daddy's sister whose life was shortened due to early onset Alzheimer's? Shame on me for not finding the time for my parents' memories and learning of relatives who are forever gone and lost to the sands of time.

I have come to the conclusion that a "Memory Porch" is a good thing. It's a room for conversation—no television allowed—for family and company just to talk. Only music is permitted—soft music. It is refreshing to have a place where memories are displayed, relived, and cherished. And children can take a trip down memory lane and learn of their ancestors of days gone by. It is a place of tears, laughter, and admonition. A porch can be a refuge for weary hearts, problematic teenagers, and weary Christians. It can also be a place where we can run away from the maddening crowd and just be still. Even Jesus did that.

Girls, stop and reflect no matter where you are or how old you are. Some rooms contribute to meditation. Our lives are so busy that few are the moments when we actually do stop . . . and just breathe . . . and think.

Take the time, my sisters. Find the Lord in these quiet moments. Go to your porch or peaceful place. Think about God and examine your relationship with Him. In fact, let's do that right now. Let's go and meet Him on the porch.

CHAPTER 9

Time To Remember You!

Do you know about "songs in the night"? Elihu spoke this phrase in Job 35:10: "But no one says, 'Where is God my Maker, Who gives songs in the night.'"

Do you find yourself contemplating spiritual things during the quiet moments of the day or perhaps at night when the house is still and you are resting? David did. Was David just an insomniac with a penchant for poetry and songs? No, Scripture teaches that David was human like us, and he constantly contemplated his need for God's deliverance, God's mercy, and God's strength, especially at nighttime when the world is quieter.

After I say my prayers at night, I crawl into bed. As I relax, I pray for the people around me, for peace to exist around me, and for the loving arms wrapped around me. I count my blessings instead of sheep. I rejoice in the absolute still of the night. Just because I no longer am kneeling and saying my nightly prayers before bedtime, my requests to God have definitely not ceased.

Time to Pray, Night and Day

Ever had one of those nights when sleep is elusive and you lie in bed, wide awake for hours? You try every relaxation method you can think of, but Mr. Sandman is a no-show. So what do you do next? You talk to the Lord. And that, my sisters, is the best conversation possible. It is absolutely imperative that we use moments like these to pray.

It is my personal opinion that our Father is often the instigator of those sleepless times. Why? Because sometimes God has to wake us up because He knows we have been too busy during the day to stop and talk to Him. We didn't seek the precious moments with Him.

Often I feel that God wants me to realize He is there, always there. I need to remember all He has done for me. So I travel down memory lane, recalling moments of God's abundant mercy, the events of my childhood, and memories of my mom, dad, and sister Judy who are now gone. I count my blessings and "name them one by one."

David lived and breathed his dependence on God and his gratitude. His praise was not limited to daylight hours. Let's look at Psalm 63. This is a wonderful song. Especially notice verse 6: "When I remember You on my bed, I meditate on You in the night watches."

Notice how David remembered God. There is certainly no absent mindedness on his part. He even thought about God "in the night watches." In Old Testament times there were three night watches: Sunset to 10:00 PM, 10:00 PM to 2:00 AM, 2:00 AM to 6:00 AM. But let's not stop there. Let's ask the question: "Why, David, are you remembering God at night?" The next line tells us: "For You [God] have been my help." And as a result, "My soul clings to You and Your right hand upholds me" (Psalm 63:7–8).

David was counting his blessings and clinging to the Lord because he had been delivered by the power of God. And be sure to notice that God's right hand held David up. Who can miss the lesson here? When we remember God's help and deliverance, this causes us to cling to our Father. And when we do, He will sustain us and hold us up.

Pause and Ponder

Copy the following scriptures on a note card, and read them every day this week. Psalm 1:2; 4:4; 119:55.

Time for God

David was a shepherd, a king, a poet, a warrior, a musician, and a prophet. With his poignant and powerful psalms, he openly describes his feelings, faults, and fears about life and his walk with God. Over and over David assures us of his personal feelings about the law of God—it is His delight. He even dedicates the longest chapter in the Bible (Psalm 119) to God's laws and testimonies. God describes David as a man after His own heart, a description said about no one else in the Bible (Acts 13:22). What a close and marvelous relationship between David and God. Do we conclude that David found the time for God? Absolutely!

How do we obtain that same kind of relationship with God? We must work on it like David did. Observe David's diligent habit of constantly praying, meditating, and studying God's law. Surely those nights spent as a shepherd on lonely and dangerous pastures caused David to turn to God, talk to Him, and trust in Him. But what is most obvious to me is that God was his top priority. Surely God has given us the truths penned by David so that we may see the relationship that's possible between God and man.

Although David did not live in our space and time, he was extremely busy running a kingdom, taking care of internal and external affairs, and staying on top of current events, not to mention having a bevy of wives and children and their constant problems that would exhaust any human. However, David's relationship with God always came first, and God blessed David powerfully for that.

God Was Always on His Mind

David's moments multiplied into a lifetime of closeness to God. With him it was never a matter of trying to squeeze God in. He walked and talked with God all hours of the day. This was David's lifestyle. And it can be our lifestyle too. Why not? What is more important than God?

Psalm 86 helps us to feel David's intense love for the Lord. Stop and read the words. I can relate very line in this psalm to my life, except the one about violent men seeking my life. (At least not yet!)

Pause and Ponder

- From Psalm 86 in your Bible: Underline every "I" statement, beginning with "I am afflicted and needy."

- Circle every "You" statement, beginning with "You, Lord, are good and ready to forgive."

- Count the "I" statements and the "You" statements. Which is greater?

Moments Invested Wisely

It is easy to see from the above exercise how David loves God and how merciful God is to him. What does it take on our part to have a good relationship with God? The main element that is required is time. It takes precious moments, sacrifice, and work. It takes choosing God and not the world.

What did Jesus teach about following Him? What was necessary? Denying oneself. "Then Jesus said to His disciples, 'If anyone wishes to come after Me, he must deny himself, and take up his cross and follow Me'" (Matthew 16:24).

We have to get ourselves and our "wants" out of the way. On his Facebook page, Trey Morgan said it so well:

> Jesus didn't pull any punches when he said, "If you want to be my disciple, you must deny yourself, take up your cross and follow me [dying to yourself]." Jesus said if you were going to follow him, you had to be all in (Luke 9:23). . . . No strings attached. He doesn't want 50 percent, 75 percent or even 95 percent of our heart and life . . . it's 100 percent . . . or nothing."

Romans 12:1–2 teaches that I must offer myself to God as a living sacrifice—not a dead one. I have only myself to give the Lord, and I must give it freely. I must choose to serve the Lord and not the world. To renew my mind means to restore it or to rejuvenate it—make it alive. How necessary that is for the Christian. I must fill my mind (the rooms inside my head) with the qualities of which my Father approves.

> Therefore I urge you, brethren, by the mercies of God, to present your bodies a living and holy sacrifice, acceptable to God, which is your spiritual service of worship. And do not be conformed to this world, but be transformed by the renewing of your mind, so that you may prove what the will of God is, that which is good and acceptable and perfect (Romans 12:1–2).

Wake Up and Smell the Coffee!

Relationships take work and sacrifice. We learn this by maturing and having friendships. If we want to walk with God, then we must first choose to walk with Him. Then we must spend time with Him, because He has become our top priority. We work on the relationship with the Father because we love Him and He loves us. The Greek philosopher Plato is credited with saying, "Human behavior flows from three main sources: desire, emotion, and knowledge." That certainly applies here. If we have a relationship with the Lord, it is because we desire it. We love Him and know what He has promised us in His mighty Word.

Look at the following insight about why we need Jesus:

> You see, when you are struggling to be who you need to be, all you have to do is look at Jesus. When you need an example of how to act in a particular situation, just look at Jesus. If you are trying to figure out if you have been living as you should in your relationships again, consider Jesus. When you ask yourself if you have already sacrificed and given enough, think about Jesus.
>
> I am so thankful Jesus came to this earth. But I am not only thankful that He died for me. I am thankful that He lived for me and continues to live for me today. He is more than just the Christ. He

is my example of living and being in this world. He is my Redeemer, my Savior, my Lord and Teacher, and my very best Friend. I need to and want to be more like Jesus. After all, isn't that the goal?[32]

Daniel

I always think of Daniel when I ponder characters of the Bible who took time for God. Carried away into Babylonian captivity, Daniel never lost His faith in God or stopped praising His name, especially to those in power.

In Daniel 6 we read of a group of satraps and commissioners who are so jealous of Daniel that they cleverly manage to have him thrown into the lions' den. Of course, we know how magnificently God delivers Daniel from the mouths of the lions, but let's focus on another aspect of the narrative.

What was the one thing Daniel did that these jealous men discovered and cleverly managed to outlaw in this Persian kingdom? Daniel prayed three times a day, and these men craftily plotted a way to use his time with God as a trap to kill him. I always wonder how they knew about Daniel's prayer life. I believe God tells us in Daniel 6:10: "In his roof chamber he had windows open toward Jerusalem." They could have seen him through those open windows, or it could be that servants had observed him praying. How remarkable is this man Daniel? Other than Jesus, who talked to God continually, we read of no one who was so faithful in prayer.

Consider the fact that Daniel was not a young man when the frameup was going on with the jealous nobles. Daniel was in his eighties, and King Darius of Persia was on the throne. How abhorrent does it seem that a group should be so jealous of an elderly righteous man in the Persian kingdom that they want him eaten by lions? And the only fault they can find is that he prays to God? Surely this was a political power struggle for this group, and Daniel stood in their way.

Pause and Ponder

🌿 Do a time line on the book of Daniel and name the kings who ruled over him. (Remember that the book of Daniel is not in chronological order.)

🌿 Read Daniel 6:10 from your Bible. Underline where Daniel prayed, how he prayed, and what he prayed.

Daniel knew the importance of talking to the Lord daily. And according to the passage above from Daniel, he also knew the importance of saying "thank you" to our God. He prayed three times every day, year in and year out, in season and out of season, in good times and tough times. It didn't matter that his life was at stake and the lion was at his door literally, Daniel was going to pray. Daniel needed God every second of the day.

Are we any different from Daniel? Are we that dedicated to talking to the Lord? Do we stop three times a day, get on our knees, and pray to the Father and thank Him?

God tells His children: "Pray without ceasing; in everything give thanks; for this is God's will for you in Christ Jesus" (1 Thessalonians 5:17–18). How interesting to note that these back-to-back verses concern the very two things that Daniel did his entire life. He prayed and gave thanks daily. This is what God wants us all to do. We are not limited to three times a day or a certain location. Praying constantly and thanking the Father continually build our relationship with Him. But just as the jealous satraps tried to ensnare Daniel, so Satan will work overtime to prevent this relationship.

Pause and Ponder

🌿 What are your thoughts on setting firm prayer times? How does one pray without ceasing?

Time to Love the Word

As this chapter began, we looked at several psalms of David, a man who wanted to please God. His attitude even affected how he responded when chastised. Remember what his first words were when he, through Nathan, understood his sin with Bathsheba? "I have sinned against the Lord" (2 Samuel 12:13). Do we too immediately repent when we have broken God's law?

Why did David talk to God regularly? Why did David think about God, write about God, and serve God so passionately? Because he loved God so much. David had an honest generous heart for God. Oh my sisters, we can have that too.

We can be wholly attuned to God as David was. We must want to. David delighted in God's Word. Read Psalm 119. Do we delight in the Bible? Is it our meditation all the day and night? Do we want to become great Bible students and sit at the feet of our Almighty God? Honestly, how important is the Bible to us? Are we daily Bible readers? Do we study and dig deeply in the Word?

If we love the Lord, we will seek precious moments to love His Word. We will read and study it. We will know it. And because of our love for the Lord, we will never stop studying His magnificent letter. Our faith will grow, grow, grow and we will change, change, change because that is what the Bible does to hearts.

The Bible Touches Hearts

If we are too busy to stop and pray, and if we are too busy to read our Father's Word, then we are just too busy.

The powerful Word of God builds our faith. "So faith comes from hearing, and hearing by the word of Christ" (Romans 10:17).

As we read and study the Bible, we read the lips of God as He inspired men to tell His story. A simple glance over its pages will never enable anyone to comprehend the magnificence of God's love. The more we read and the more we study the Bible, the more we see the entire picture of God's plan for mankind to be saved, from Genesis to Revelation. God openly and very honestly lets us see the good, the bad, and the ugly of events which strengthen our daily walk. His word is always relevant.

My heart breaks when I read about the immorality and the idolatry of God's people in the Old Testament. Over and over God blessed them, then punished them, and then delivered them. The children of Israel disappointed God repeatedly. Let's read Jeremiah 6:16, one of the most heart-wrenching passages in the entire Bible: "Thus says the Lord, 'Stand by the ways and see and ask for the ancient paths, where the good way is, and walk in it; and you will find rest for your souls. But they said, 'We will not walk in it.'"

Can any of us possibly imagine hearing God tell us how to live and die rightly, and then our saying to Him, "I won't do it"? How could anyone say that to our Father? But God's children—not the enemy's children but God's children—did. What gall! Let's also remember that even though His children rejected Him, God still loved them. God still kept His promise and sent Jesus to die for the world. How do you describe such wondrous love? See how the Bible touches hearts?

Pause and Ponder

Examine the phrase "rest for your souls" from Jeremiah 6:16. Find another scripture containing these words. Who is speaking?

God's Memory Porch

God wants us to remember Him. When we're into His word, we are inside His memory porch. From times of old, He instituted days and feasts for His children to recall His power and mighty works.

In the Old Testament the feasts that God commanded His people to observe reminded Israel of His deliverance and love. Think of the Passover and how God brought His people out of Egypt. Think of the

Feast of Pentecost, a feast to remind the Jews of God's call to holiness at Sinai. Think of the Feast of Booths to renew the covenant God made with Israel at Sinai. Although God did not command the Jews to remember Esther with a feast, the Jews observed the Feast of Purim.

In this age, we observe the memorial of the Lord's supper. Every Sunday we gather with the family of God and remember the body and the blood of Jesus, broken and poured out for us. We recall Jesus, His life, His death, and His resurrection. We have bound the cross and the empty tomb upon our hearts and minds. Nothing is more sober, serious, meaningful, or contemplative. We are determined that we shall never forget Jesus, as this most important memory of all is the essence of our life as a Christian.

May we never forget that it is our holy and gracious God who gives us a mind in which to store memories. Take care of your mind, my sister. Be careful what you store there.

The Bible has the power to touch our hearts and make us love our God more and more. The Bible helps us to grow up, but spiritual maturity will never occur if God's Word is rarely opened. God knows where He is on our priority list—the top or the bottom or somewhere in between. He knows all and is never fooled. He knows what we do with our time.

What Will We Do?

What will we do today with Jesus' invitation, "Come to Me, all who are weary and heavy-laden, and I will give you rest" (Matthew 11:28)? Thousands of years ago, God's children mockingly told Him no. Will we wear their sandals, dress like them, think like them, and repeat the very same thing to Jesus today?

God's Word, the Bible, is our instruction book to bless our lives and then save our souls at the end of time. And believe it or not, there are quite a few of us who think about our destiny and our salvation during the day and even in the middle of the night like David did. We faithfully discover new meanings, new concepts, and heart-stabbing, life-changing accounts in God's Word.

Only God could have written this Book and told these stories. Only God. That task was impossible for a human. *It's up to us to find time for God, Jesus, and the Holy Spirit.* Open the Book and read, learn, obey, and grow. It could not be any simpler.

> Our physical growth stops at some point, usually during our teen years. Our growth plates have fused and there is no potential or possibility for further growth. The wonderful thing about our spiritual growth is that there is no ending point. We can expect to continue to develop as we study, pray, and interact regularly with fellow Christians. Our physical growth happens regardless of any desire for growth on our part. A child doesn't consciously decide to grow or to stop growing. God has genetically programmed his development, and regardless of a child's wishes, he will grow. Spiritual growth doesn't happen in that manner. It won't happen without conscious effort on our part. We have to want to develop and grow spiritually and seek opportunities to promote that spiritual growth.[33]

Christ tells us to come to Him (choose Him), take His yoke (surrender and live Christlike), and learn (get biblical knowledge) from Him so that we will find rest (have forgiveness of sins and a promise of a future in heaven). These are all actions verbs turned into action commands, and every one of them takes effort on our part. Come, take, and learn. It is imperative for us to daily remind ourselves of Jesus' words, "My yoke is easy and My burden is light."

> It only remains to inquire, "How may men take Christ's yoke upon them?" This is done, as he said, by those who "learn" of him. That refers to hearing, believing, repenting, confessing, being baptized, and walking in all the commandments and ordinances of the Lord. People take Christ's yoke upon them by obeying the gospel and taking up their full duties and obligations in the church which is Christ's body. That such is surely a burden or "yoke," none may deny; but it is a burden which makes all other burdens light.[34]

I believe this scripture in Matthew 11:28–30 is one of the best when it comes to calming the soul and giving peace all hours of the day, but especially on a sleepless night. Look at it one more time.

> Come to Me, all who are weary and heavy-laden, and I will give you rest. Take My yoke upon you and learn from Me, for I am gentle and humble in heart, and you will find rest for your souls. For My yoke is easy and My burden is light.

All who are weary and heavy-laden. In my Bible, the words "weary and heavy-laden" literally mean "who work to exhaustion." Ah, now we get it. We really understand this comfort passage because it speaks to so many of us who work to exhaustion. Remember our theme song: I am woman, hear me gasp!

"Come to Me, all who work to exhaustion, and I will give you rest." Rest for our souls.

MOMENTS IN PRAYER

Oh, Father, thank You for Jesus and the rest that we find only in Him. Please help us never to forget Your Word and to be dedicated to it. Thank You for the marvelous memories in the Bible, and help us to change our lives to please You. Lord, help us find the time to remember You and to be a pleasing daughter. In Jesus' name, Amen.

Moments in Song

"In the Hush of Early Morning" and "Lord, Take Control"

KEEP SEEKING

1. How important is the Bible to you? Why?
2. What do you do on sleepless nights?

3. What is there about God's narrative of Daniel that amazes you?
4. What Bible stories are your favorites?

66 Timely Quotes 99

"I wish I had a mind so narrow that it would
hold only those things I know of God."
—Jim Gardner

"We must use time as a tool, not as a crutch."
—John F. Kennedy

"Lost time is never found again."
—Benjamin Franklin

"You're going to meet an old woman some day. She may be a seasoned, soft, gracious lady, a gentlewoman who has grown old gracefully, surrounded by a host of friends. Or she may be a bitter, disillusioned, dried up, cynical woman without a good word for anybody—soured, friendless, and alone.

"The kind of old woman you meet depends entirely on yourself, because that old woman will be you. She will be the composite of everything you do, say, and think today and tomorrow. Her mind will be set in a mold you have made by your attitudes. Her heart will be turning out what you have been putting in. . . . Every day in every way you are becoming more and more like yourself."
—Richard C. Halverson, from Facebook

A Letter from Jeff And Angela

I recently asked our son and his wife, Jeff and Angela, to write about their inner feelings concerning Jeff's choice to add "preacher" to his job description. Our son and his family live in the Texas panhandle and have owned and operated several newspapers there. About a year ago, the elders in Wheeler, Texas, asked Jeff to consider being their full-time preacher. Because I want this book to relate to younger Christians, their time for God, and their point of view on God and His church, I am including their stories.

FROM JEFF

Back in 2008 when I was thirty-two years old, Angela and I lived in Lubbock, Texas. Our third child, Eva, had just been born. We attended church regularly and I loved being a part of the church there. I really had to stand my ground about that congregation when it came to my family.

I realize now that I felt compelled to attend there because I really needed to grow up spiritually, and that is where I began to grow and challenge my beliefs. I think God put us in that church for a reason.

I remember one really frustrating Sunday. Angela and I were talking about worship, and I was really bothered by something that happened during worship. My wife, who is very patient with me spiritually, told me I really was acting immature and unreasonable about ridiculous things. She also pointed out I was judging my fellow Christians, and that I needed to be very careful talking in not so flattering terms about my church family.

She wisely pointed out that I simply wasn't focusing on Jesus. At some point in my walk, I really had lost sight of that. My really immature reaction to the

160

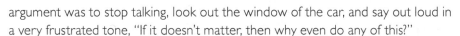

argument was to stop talking, look out the window of the car, and say out loud in a very frustrated tone, "If it doesn't matter, then why even do any of this?"

Silence.

What's worse is, I was serious. After about a minute I realized I had a problem. A big problem. As President Trump would say, *huge* problem. At that moment I knew Satan had me; I was a weak Christian. He had talked me into just giving it all up. Like many other Christians I've seen in my lifetime, I was ready to pick up my toys like a child and leave and never play again. I was ready to jettison my faith, because everything at worship that morning didn't go just like I thought it should go. At that moment, I was ready to quit it all.

Where was my faith? What exactly did I have faith in? It certainly wasn't in Jesus Christ. I had to come to the realization that my faith was in "punching my time card" and not in my Savior. I say that honestly, and I realize that was a "me" problem. My parents had done a great job raising me to be a faithful Christian; however, I really hadn't done any growing in a long time. Decades. The fact that it took me so long to see that is depressing.

Growing up, I was very much about doing things as I was shown to do them by my incredibly faithful family, which is fantastic. But my problem is that I just relied on my family's faith, and I didn't take the time to grow my own. This is tough to confess, but I feel like we all have our own struggles, and we have them for a reason.

We sometimes believe as we do because everyone around us believes that way. That was me. I'd never questioned anything I was taught from scripture. In fact, I felt that questioning the basics of faith was forbidden and unacceptable. I accepted what I was told as truth. I was not like the noble Bereans who searched the scriptures daily to see if what Paul was saying was true. Instead I was very much from the "I am of Apollos" or "I am of Paul" crowd. I was happy to rest on other people's faith and draw a little faith from it. I had to admit to myself that I was a shallow Christian. Ouch! It made for a really long Sunday!

I was a late bloomer when I obeyed the gospel—almost fifteen. That's ancient when it comes to growing up in the church. My immature reason was that I didn't feel like I'd ever really done anything majorly wrong in my life. Really?

It wasn't until that one Sunday night at Forest Park Church of Christ in Georgia, when local preacher Bill Denton was preaching about becoming a Christian, that I finally realized that I was lost and that I did have sin in my life. That night I did obey the gospel and check that box off. Unfortunately I didn't grow much from there.

So I was able to hang in there with my spiritual immaturity through college and through the beginning of my marriage, but the cracks really began to show through in Lubbock. It was apparent to my wife, who has the most amazing faith I've ever known, and it was becoming apparent to my young children.

I had to make a choice to grow spiritually or die spiritually. There really isn't an in between. I needed to figure out why being a Christian was important to me, and my answer couldn't be because of my Christian heritage. It couldn't just be because I went to church every time the doors were open. I had to find a deeper meaning to why I was a Christian.

I'm happy to say that through the next ten years my family was able to be a part of some incredible congregation. I've learned what it means to love a God who loves me so much that He gave His Son for me.

Those years have helped me realize what this church business is about. It's about service; it's about God's unrelenting love for His creation that is so tangled up in sin; it's about wanting to look like Jesus and to act like He did when He was here. And most important, it's about seeking and saving the lost. It's also about having this thirst to study and learn more about His Word and find out more and more about Him.

Once you figure that out, there isn't a question anymore of whether or not you're going to be there when the doors are open, or if you'll participate in church activities. You will because His church means everything. It's the Bride of Christ, purchased at an awesome price, the cost of Jesus' blood. I owe Him everything, and I love being a part of His church.

I suddenly wanted everyone else to feel the same way I did.

It took me a while to figure what being a Christian really means. I realized why a couple of Oklahomans—my grandparents, Russ and Lea Fowler—living in Marlow, Oklahoma, in the 1950s packed their family up and moved to New England and started teaching others about Jesus Christ and the church He died for. I now understood why my parents were so adamant that my that sister and I be faithful members of the church of Christ. So taking the preaching job last year was a big change, but it was an easy choice.

I made the choice because I really felt like I wasn't serving God as He wished by staying on the sidelines. I felt, "It's time to step into the pulpit, and whatever happens from there is in God's hands." Angela was part of that choice; she encouraged me. I'm thankful to say I took that step and that my wife and I made that decision on our own.

For those out there on the fence who have had the same type of struggles, the view is great from this side of the fence. Come on over. Satan wants you content and comfortable. Shake things up. It'll drive him crazy if you change your life for the cause of Jesus Christ.

FROM ANGELA

Being a preacher's wife is not something I ever set out to be, but being married to a Christian man who loves the Lord and follows His leading is something I hoped and prayed for always.

It has been quite a journey to this point in our lives. We have been through many struggles and triumphs in our short nineteen years of marriage, and I know that the adventure will continue.

My faith has only grown stronger each step of the way. Looking back, I can see God's providential hand guiding us and correcting us all along the path we have traveled. It's not easy seeing where His hand is leading in the little things that happen each day. We don't understand why things happen the way they do, but when you look back at the big picture, it all makes perfect sense.

I'm so thankful for Christ's church and His family, which is my family, and even more so now that Jeff is a preacher. I continually ask myself, what would we do without them? No matter what our earthly occupations are, His church is where we belong.

Grandchildren:
Wil Blackmon, Lex Stewart, Nora
Balckmon, Max Stewart, Eva Blackmon

CHAPTER 10

Time To Take Off Your Shoes!

o we fully appreciate God's holiness? Scrutinize the following comments about the scribes' rituals when they wrote God's name:

> A scribe would wash his hands, and work diligently to be certain of mistake free, and beautiful work. Early Hebrew scribes would even take a bath, put on fresh clean clothes, and make a new pen, when writing the name of God."[35]

These scribes revered God and recognized the Scriptures as holy, pure, and righteous.

The Bible comes from the very mouth of God. It is God breathed. The verses below are "must" memory verses for God's children:

> 2 Timothy 3:16–17—"All Scripture is inspired by God and profitable for teaching, for reproof, for correction, for training in righteousness, so that the man of God may be adequate, equipped for every good work."

> 2 Peter 1:20–21—"But know this first of all, that no prophecy of Scripture is a matter of one's own interpretation, for no prophecy

was ever made by an act of human will, but men moved by the Holy Spirit spoke from God."

Matthew 4:4—Jesus said to Satan in the wilderness, "It is written, 'Man shall not live on bread alone, but on every word that proceeds out of the mouth of God.'"

Time in a Holy Place

What is it like to be where God is? Do we wonder about that? I think the experience would be wonderful and also terrifying. God told Moses, "Do not come near here; remove your sandals from your feet, for the place on which you are standing is holy ground" (Exodus 3:5). And Moses obeyed God.

Joshua experienced something very familiar when the captain of the Lord's host said to him, "Remove your sandals from your feet, for the place where you are standing is holy" (Joshua 5:15). And Joshua did so.

Somehow, I cannot see Moses or Joshua telling God, "I just don't have the time to stop and chat. You've got thirty minutes and then I'm out of here."

God tells us what happened to Moses' face when He spoke with him.

It came about when Moses was coming down from Mount Sinai (and the two tablets of the testimony were in Moses' hand as he was coming down from the mountain), that Moses did not know that the skin of his face shone because of his speaking with Him (Exodus 34:29).

Being in the presence of God changed Moses' appearance. Being in the presence of God changes every man.

What happened in the New Testament when people encountered angels? They were frightened, some almost scared to death. Let's look at these passages:

Now after the Sabbath, as it began to dawn toward the first day of the week, Mary Magdalene and the other Mary came to look at the grave. And behold, a severe earthquake had occurred, for an angel of the Lord descended from heaven and came and rolled away the stone and sat upon it. And his appearance was like lightning, and his clothing as white as snow. The guards shook for fear of him and became like dead men (Matthew 28:1–4).

Entering the tomb, they saw a young man sitting at the right, wearing a white robe; and they were amazed. And he said to them, "Do not be amazed; you are looking for Jesus the Nazarene, who has been crucified. He has risen; He is not here; behold, here is the place where they laid Him. But go, tell His disciples and Peter, 'He is going ahead of you to Galilee; there you will see Him, just as He told you.'" They went out and fled from the tomb, for trembling and astonishment had gripped them; and they said nothing to anyone, for they were afraid (Mark 16:5–8).

And an angel of the Lord appeared to him, standing to the right of the altar of incense. Zacharias was troubled when he saw the angel, and fear gripped him (Luke 1:11–12).

 Pause and Ponder

What was the reaction of mortals in the presence of holy ones? Underline the answers in the above verses. How does James 2:19 describe the response of demons to God?

Journey back in time to that magnificent day when the Jews from the Babylonian captivity finally gathered again in Jerusalem. And Ezra read from God's Word.

Ezra opened the book in the sight of all the people for he was standing above all the people; and when he opened it, all the people stood up. Then Ezra blessed the Lord the great God. And all the people answered, "Amen! Amen!" while lifting up their hands; then they bowed low and worshiped the Lord with their faces to the ground (Nehemiah 8:5–6).

How did the people react to God's Word being opened? They stood up; they bowed down and worshiped Him. The refugees showed their respect for God and His Word.

The Challenge of Holiness

What do we know about those who are before the throne of God? John was inspired to write about them in the book of Revelation: "Day and night they do not cease to say, "Holy, holy, holy is the Lord God, the Almighty, who was and who is and who is to come" (Revelation 4:8).

It is essential that we understand the enormity of being in the presence of God as we read and handle His powerful Word. We're aware of Jehovah God, the Almighty God, El Shaddai, El Adonai, and Yahweh every time we open the Bible! Across the pages of His magnificent book, our Creator speaks to each of us personally. He has a life-changing message to tell, and who will listen? Will you? Will I?

Will we mock the law of God and "sit in the seat of scoffers" (Psalm 1:1)? Do we grasp the concept of God being with us as we worship every Sunday? This is serious business as we realize we are on holy ground.

Time for the Whole Bible

Do we read only certain books of the Bible? True, some books are tough for every Bible student to handle. When we read difficult passages and hard-to-understand books such as Leviticus, Numbers, Daniel, and Revelation, what do we do? What should we do when it comes to reading the tribes, their offspring's names, and the numbers of men? Let's recall that God has a reason for putting them in His Word.

I have heard Christians foolishly say, "Oh, I just skip those chapters and books. I don't understand them and some describe diseases that are gross!" Girls, there are many things we don't understand about the Bible, but please keep plugging away. These words are from God, right? Then be the grownup who attempts to meet the person with a difficult name. You just might meet him in person some day. Stop and contemplate the numerical size of each tribe. Look at the diseases and unclean objects God wanted His people to avoid. God intends for us to learn lesson after lesson. Who are we to say they are not important?

Remember, God does not think like we do, so read the numbers and the names. We cannot pick and choose which passages are important and which are not. To attempt to do so is what some call "cafeteria religion." All are important because God spoke them into existence. Don't ask why, just keep on reading. If it was important enough for God to inspire a man to write it down, then that's all we need to know. End of story.

Time to Ask

Ask questions as you read. Explore the cultures and societies in the background of the passage you are studying. He wants His children to know Him and not be ignorant. Do research on scriptures and discover the history and geography from commentary writers, and you will have those light bulb moments when you say, "Oh, now I get it!" And when you do this, my sisters, you have just climbed up one more rung on the ladder of Christian maturity. You will experience a unique excitement because you understand more about your Father.

Remember the relatives' photos on Mom's memory porch? Let's be the daughter who wants to know about all the relatives. Look at the people that God names and realize that they are family. Ask questions. They are real people who led real lives and were God's children just like you and me.

Surely our Father wants His children to meet and know one another, even this side of heaven. I may not have a picture of Merari or Nahshon to look at, but God has given me a picture of words describing these two in Numbers 2 and 3 who had roles in packing up the tabernacle and leading the army of Israel.

I want to meet Achsah, the daughter of Caleb, who was one smart cookie who asked her father for more than just real estate. She asked him for the most treasured object in the Palestinian world: water. Pretty bold, intelligent, and brave I would say.

Pause and Ponder

What did Achsah ask of her father (Joshua 15:18–19)?

God's One Liners

It takes only one verse for God to describe something intriguing and leave you wanting more. Judges 20 is amazing, recounting a time of civil war among God's people. Seven hundred choice men from the tribe of Benjamin were "left-handed; every one could sling a stone at a hair and not miss" (Judges 20:16). Every time I read this, I visualize what fantastic baseball and tennis players these Benjamites would have made. But God did not make these men skillful to excel at sports but so they could kill animals and men swiftly and unexpectedly.

I love reading about Zeruiah, sister of David. She was the mother of three unusual sons: Abishai, Joab, and Asahel. Do you know these three men and their fascinating stories? Go and find them—they'll knock your socks off. Not a lot of women are mentioned in the Old Testament, but God surely mentions Zeruiah amidst all the names in 1 Chronicles 2. However, it takes work to find her.

The same goes for the prayer of Jabez which was very popular years ago. Tucked away in 1 Chronicles 4:10, we see the plea from Jabez to God for protection, blessings, and land. And God said yes. Haven't we asked God for these same things too? Oh, the lessons to be learned about prayer right there. What amazing things God can teach us in just one verse!

Pause and Ponder

Using your Bible dictionary, report on one of Zeruiah's sons: Abishai, Joab, or Asahel.

Someone once said, "The Bible is the only book whose author is present when one is reading it." Let us remember that. If only we will take precious moments to dig deeply and discover the powerful teachings and examples there. Allow God to do His work. There is so much to be learned, and God blesses those who seek Him in His Word.

Stop, Look, and Listen

Most of us learned the pedestrian rule: Stop, look, and listen. When we are walking with traffic zooming, we need to pay attention. What about when we're walking through the Word? We need to stop, look, and listen to see what God is telling us. Let's examine every verse we possibly can and dig for clarity and background. Do character studies. Get to know the relatives and where they lived.

Get in the Word. You will be seeking the precious moments. And you'll be ready for the Lord to come at any moment. Be the wise servant Jesus mentioned.

> Who then is the faithful and sensible slave whom his master put in charge of his household to give them their food at the proper time? Blessed is that slave whom his master finds so doing when he comes (Matthew 24:45–46).

Wayne Jackson has this to say about the above passage:

> What are the traits of the "faithful and wise servant" whom the Lord has appointed to administer his affairs? He is the one the Master finds active when he unexpectedly arrives.[36]

To me, *active* means "awake, alive, doing, and participating." That is a description of the Christian. Let's look at the opposite of this scripture. Does the Lord say, "Blessed is that slave whom his master finds doing nothing when he comes"? Of course not. How was this servant described by Jesus? Two adjectives: *faithful* and *wise.* Each of us must do a self-examination and ask, "Would Jesus describe me as having those two marvelous qualities?"

Honor the Father; Take Off Your Shoes

I am in awe of Almighty God, aren't you? If so, then find the time to thank Him for His mercies and honor Him daily. Do the sunrise and the sunset take your breath away? Tell Him. And how about the ocean or a mountain range? Talk to Him again. Tell Him you love His creation, for He loves it too. Work on the relationship.

Look at what Jane McWhorter wrote in her book, *Roses in December*:

> Evidence of the culmination of His awareness of beauty may be found at the conclusion of the sixth day in Genesis 1:31: "Then God saw everything that He had made, and indeed it was very good." God's day-by-day awareness of the beauty of the world around Him should be a wake-up call for all of us to open our eyes and notice the preciousness of everyday life.[37]

Pause and Ponder

Read the following poem by Elizabeth Barrett Browning:

> Earth's crammed with heaven,
> And every common bush afire with God,
> But only he who sees takes off his shoes;
> The rest sit round and pluck blackberries.

Which one are you? Are you a "seer" or a "sitter"? Do you see God all around you, or do you just sit, eat, and take every blessing for granted—especially God? Have you removed your shoes?

What Does God Want?

What is God's will for us? He wants us to be saved. He wants us to be with Him in heaven. He wants us to know the truth. He wants us to know Him. "This is good and acceptable in the sight of God our Savior, who desires all men to be saved and to come to the knowledge of the truth" (1 Timothy 2:3–4).

> Thus says the Lord, "Let not a wise man boast of his wisdom, and let not the mighty man boast of his might, let not a rich man boast of his riches; but let him who boasts boast of this, that he understands and knows Me, that I am the Lord who exercises lovingkindness, justice and righteousness on earth; for I delight in these things," declares the Lord (Jeremiah 9:23–24).

God wants us to seek Him, His will, and His truth. How and where will we find these precious entities? There is only one revealing place, and that is His Word. The Bible has all the answers, the first word and the last word. "The Bible is the perfect and complete will of God. It is the anvil that breaks the hammers. It is the standard by which we will be judged when Jesus comes again."[38] Most of all, it is the only book that will get us home to the Father.

David expressed it like this: "Seek the Lord and His strength; seek His face continually. Remember His wonders which He has done, His marvels and the judgments uttered by His mouth" (Psalm 105:4–5).

The Top Most Requested DVDs

It should not be a surprise to Christians that the world wants to know God too. The world is curious about Him, and many seek Him and ask questions. The Bible continues to be one of the most popular books in bookstores. The world is intrigued by God, even if they do not obey Him.

The World Video Bible School in Maxwell, Texas, sends out hundreds of DVDs every month to people all over the world who want more information about God. Their mission is to spread Jesus' gospel to the four corners of the earth. There are thousands who visit the website daily where WVBS livestreams free soul-saving lessons by preachers and teachers: www.wvbs.org. Guess what the top two most requested DVDs are from all over the world: "Searching for Truth" and "Where Do We Go When We Die?"

Don't ever think that no one is interested in finding God. My sisters, our never-ending work for the Lord goes on. Many souls need to be saved. We must never believe that no one wants to hear the good news of Jesus anymore. Satan wants us to think that the gospel is obsolete and that no one cares about God. That's not true.

Righteous Souls in Wicked Places

Even the worldliest cities hold souls who want to know God. Consider what God said about Corinth.

> And the Lord said to Paul in the night by a vision, "Do not be afraid any longer, but go on speaking and do not be silent; for I am with you, and no man will attack you in order to harm you, for I have many people in this city." And he settled there a year and six months, teaching the word of God among them (Acts 18:9–11).

Paul may have been fearful that the persecution he experienced from town to town would happen in Corinth, which it eventually did. But God had a plan for Paul, the people in Corinth, and the church of Corinth, a horribly immoral city. He allowed Paul to preach and teach there for eighteen months. I imagine that one reason God allowed Paul to stay there so long was because such a wicked place needed a righteous man like Paul.

And who was more wicked than Jezebel and her followers in Israel? Elijah ran from her when she sought to kill him. Then he holed up in a cave and the Lord asked him twice, "What are you doing here, Elijah?"

Pause and Ponder

Read 1 Kings 19:13–18 and summarize Elijah's answer to God's question.

Elijah had just come from a triumphant display of God's magnificence on Mount Carmel and the contest between Baal's priests and God. And still Elijah, the great prophet whom God later took home in a whirlwind, ran from a queen, showing a lack of faith in the God who had just delivered him. But what did God tell this mighty man? In essence God told him, "I still have work for you to do. You've got to anoint a new king. You've also got to anoint a new prophet who will take your place. And besides all that, there are seven thousand people who are not worshiping Baal. Get out of that cave and get on with serving Me!"

We must never give up. As long as there are souls on the earth, there will be a need for a Savior and a need for vessels like us who will go and teach the gospel. Let's give ourselves a pep talk, get out of whatever cave is holding us back, and get on with serving our God. My precious sisters, who will go and work for Him today? Don't look back—just up!

Pause and Ponder

Research the hymn, "My House Is Full," by Lanny Wolfe. What lines are especially meaningful to you?

MOMENTS IN PRAYER

Oh Lord, we love You with all our heart. Thank You for Your constant love and protection. Lord, help us to read Your word more carefully and diligently. Help us to love our family that You reveal there. Help us to slow down. Lord, please help us to find the time to respect You and Your Word. But Lord, most of all, help us to go and teach the lost in this world. In Jesus' name, Amen.

 Moments in Song

"We Are Standing on Holy Ground" and "We Praise Thee, O God"

KEEP SEEKING

1. Even though we cannot have Moses' experience of holy ground, what experiences bring us closer to God?
2. How can we renew or restore our minds?
3. Why do you think there are still people in the world who want to hear the gospel?

 Timely Quotes

"Time is not measured by the years that we live, but by the deeds that we do and the joys that we give."
—Helen Steiner Rice

"Everybody has a chapter they don't read out loud."
—Anonymous, from JustLifeQuotes

Home Sweet Home

How many of you remember those homemade samplers that hung on the wall in days gone by? Sometimes they were quotes from the Bible or just famous short thoughts to pique our interest. They were usually cross-stitched and occasionally had landscape scenes on the canvas. Today they are quite collectible, especially the ones from the early beginnings of our nation.

I was nine years old when my family decided to move to New England to do mission work. My mom loved the antiques that were so plentiful in the northeast in those days. Antiquing became her thing.

Frequently we would fly down the road—that's the way Mom drove—and come to a screeching halt as she saw those magic signs: "Barn Sale" or "Antiques Inside." Seat belts were nonexistent back in those days, so when Mom had to stop suddenly, the only safety belt was the back of her hand as it flew across the seat and caught me right under my chin. Her hand saved me from hitting the dashboard many a time. And it worked because I still have my teeth, just barely. My dad used to say, "Your mom only knows one speed—floorboard." But I digress.

Back to the antiques. When our family stopped at one of these junky treasure-ridden shops, my mom would look at us three kids and say, "You have two choices. Either stay in the car and behave or come inside with me and get an education." Since I was the youngest and knew the fate that awaited me in the car, I chose the latter. I am so glad that I did.

Antique proprietors are usually endowed with great knowledge and are eager to answer any questions, even from children. New Englanders especially love the idea of education and knowledge, and they willingly offer their expertise to those who want to know more, whether it be antiques, cars, or whatever. All you have to do is ask. So I started asking and looking. One particular time, a store owner answered all my questions about how to tell cut glass from pressed glass and insisted that I take three small cut glass bowls home with me. A curious mind does pay off.

Somehow a pretty little sampler appeared in my bedroom when we lived in Vermont. It simply said: "Home Is Where Your Heart Is." I loved to lie in bed and gaze at its simplicity and loveliness. I often wondered, "Who made this? And how could she let it go?"

My family moved to New Hampshire and wound up staying in New England thirty years. Wherever we moved, that little sampler traveled too. It lived in my room. When I was going to leave home and get married, I asked my mother if I could take that special sampler with me. How could she refuse? I happily tucked it in my suitcase, and it wound up in my new life in Atlanta, quite a distance for that lovely little northern piece of fine stitchery to journey.

I am telling you this because that precious sampler was comfort for me. It didn't matter where I was, it gave me security simply by being there. "Home Is Where Your Heart Is." Whether my room was located in New Hampshire or Georgia, it didn't matter. My heart could move along with my belongings.

I also came to realize that the very essence of home was not a house or any structure. In the beginning, home was where my parents were, where our little family laughed and loved. As a young bride and mother, that little sampler soon described a new chapter in my life and even expanded its perimeters. My heart now was with my Jeff, as well as the family that was growing up around me. My parents were a definite part of that. Home was simply where we all loved each other. Home was where all of our hearts gathered together. Home was not a house.

I don't know about you, my friend, but there is nothing sweeter than being part of a family and loving them. Now I would certainly be living in "la-la land" if I told you that every family is perfect. There is no perfect family. We all have our faults, and home is where nobody is fooled. The masks are dropped. We know what buttons to push with each other. Sometimes family is a real zoo, or perhaps a circus or a prison.

Adam and Eve once dwelt in a perfect paradise. But when Satan and sin entered the picture, everything changed. And it changed for everyone from that moment on. No more walking with the Lord in the cool of the evening. Instead there was hard work, painful childbirth, jealousy, rivalry, lying, murder, and more.

The very first couple experienced every parent's fear: the death of a child. Surely Adam and Eve reflected on their own family life as they buried Abel, a son murdered by his brother Cain. What went through your mind, Eve, as you held Abel for the last time, if you were able to do that? Adam, did you agonize over all the lost opportunities and the what ifs? How their hearts must have been overflowing with grief, heartbreak, and sorrow as they stood beside his grave. Perhaps we feel their pain as we imagine what the first funeral was like for that first family.

I will always be enchanted by old-fashioned samplers. To tell you the truth, I am mighty partial to any kind of sign that describes love in a home. One quote that is a treasure hangs in our hall: "Our family is a circle of strength. With every birth and every union, the circle grows. Every crisis faced together makes the circle stronger."

What makes a home a home is not all the good times. What makes a home a home is all the good and the bad, the suffering, the laughter, the tears, the memories, and the love that abides there. Not perfectness, just love and forgiveness.

There is nothing like family. We all need a place that we know will always be there, even when Satan has made a total wreck of our lives. Mom was once captivated by a sign reading: "Home Is Where They Have to Take You In."

We don't know what tomorrow will bring. Make time for family. Love one another. Let your heart expand and welcome others into your precious family, because so many have no family. Hold each other close, and don't let go. There will be moments soon enough when you would give anything to experience that embrace one more time or hear that voice one more time, but the one you love has flown away.

CHAPTER 11

Time to Love That Family!

All you have to do is say the word *family*, and you've got my attention. And you have everybody else's attention too. Why is that? Because the family and home mean absolutely everything to most people. Talk about family and you are hitting Ol' Beck where she loves and lives. Ask any mama how her kids are, and you will be stuck in a two-hour detailed conversation. Criticize a woman's children, and you have a battle on your hands. We women are grizzly bears when it comes to our young.

Family is a word that describes the people inside our home—parents, siblings, and grandparents. Family makes a place a home. Home is our nest where we grow up, where we settle in to do nothing or do something, where those we love are around us, and where we find peace and respite from the world. Or that should be home. Realistically, we know that not every home has love and peace in it. The Hal David/Burt Bacharach song, "A House Is Not a Home," describes that concept well.

Pause and Ponder

Research the Hal David/Burt Bacharach song, "A House Is Not a Home," and discuss it. How does a loveless home affect the children?

🌿 Examine the following quote: "You don't choose your family. They are God's gift to you, as you are to them" (Desmond Tutu).

🌿 Discuss times when the last sentence may not be true.

A home should be filled with kisses. Maybe you've heard that home is where they have to take you in. Home is our place to love, eat, relax, refresh, laugh, argue, forgive, and love some more. Masks are dropped, and the persons that we really are—our deep-down souls—dwell there. Family also consists of those whom we love, but interestingly enough, these people are also the very same people who know just what buttons to push to make us jealous, angry, spiteful—and loving. Right? I see you nodding your head. You know how to get your brother going, and vice versa. Our God-given emotions can certainly erupt after skillful prodding by the people we love the most, especially at family get togethers. Billy Carter, the brother of President Jimmy Carter, once remarked, "We don't have family reunions in our family. There would be at least two homicides!" I totally get that.

Several years ago when the Persian Gulf War was in full swing, military troops were being sent back and forth across the ocean. A network's reporter was interviewing a soldier, and he truthfully said, "I can't wait to get home where I can just be myself again." A place to just be yourself. That probably is the best description of home and family there is.

As I said in an earlier chapter, I love most of the signs that are popular now. I have one in my office that says this:

In Our Home

We do faithful.	We do mistakes.
We do happiness.	We do love.
We do I'm sorry.	We do hugs.
We do dreams.	We do loud really well.
We do laughter.	We do family.
We do real.	We do thank you.
We do second chances.	We do grace.

No home is perfect. No family is perfect. *Dysfunctional* is a word that can apply to many of us because perhaps we grew up in a home where nothing was normal. Not every home has two parents. Not every two-parent home has two happy parents. And some homes have only one parent who is trying to be "all things to all people." That's not hard—that's tough!

Here is a sad list from a Facebook post, credited to some foster child. It is unfortunate that many, many children could have written such a list.

Things I Want in My Family

I want food and water.

Don't hit on me.

A house with running
water and lights.

I want love.

Mom and Dad—
don't fight.

I want no drugs.

Don't kill my pets.

Help with school.

Nice clean clothes.

No lice. No
bug in house.

Clean house.

Clean bed with covers.

Don't sell my toys.

Treated fair.

Don't get drunk.

TV in house.

Let me keep my games.

School stuff.

Nice shoes.

My own comb.

Soap.

Nice house and safe

AC and heater.

Coat.

Toothbrush.

Maybe someone you know experienced that childhood. Many of us cannot read that list without thanking the Father for our childhood, our parents, and the blessings we had. Oh, how easy it is to take our blessings for granted. One thing I noticed about this list is how much this child desired something clean. Clean house, clean bed, water, and soap. The absolute basics. Girls, when we read a heart-wrenching letter like this, we may not know the child, but we surely can do something.

We can pray for that child and for those like her. God knows where all the hurting children live. We may never meet half the people we pray for, but pray anyway and let God handle it.

Pause and Ponder

How can the situation written by this foster child be prevented? Find at least two scriptures that show how the Lord is on the side of children.

Endless Beginning

My dad used to say, "When you have a child, you have started something you will never finish." That's true, because you will never live long enough to see all the offspring that will be produced by your own children, their children, and their children's children. Bringing a baby into this world is exciting and mind boggling, to say the least. The United States Department of Agriculture has stated, "For a middle-income family to raise a child born in 2015 through the age of seventeen, the cost has hit $233,610."[39] Naturally, this figure continually increases due to the escalating cost of living.

From the moment a baby comes into a family, life changes for the couple. Life is turned upside down, and everything in that household revolves around the child—its nourishment, religious upbringing, physical and mental health, education, friends, clothes, and such like. The home that consisted of only two people has now become a family.

Perhaps more children are born into this family. Now the parents must cope and quickly adjust to a new norm, a life where the logistics have changed again. Being a parent is never easy. It is quite stressful, to be honest. Being ready for the multitude of problems that can occur daily requires constant prayer and help from the Father of all fathers.

Having siblings is a good thing for a child, and rivalry will occur. That is natural. Children have to figure out where they fit in the fabric of their family. I can still hear my mother's voice ringing out on so many occasions: "Rebecca Lea, the world does *not* revolve around you!" I had to learn that she was right.

No matter how we look at it, having a child is a wondrous thing. Holding a sleeping baby or rocking a sick child fills our heart with inexpressible feelings. I thought I knew love when I was young. Then I had a baby; then a grandbaby. Now I know another dimension of love.

Barbara Bush once said, "To us, family means putting your arms around each other and being there." As parents we often try to provide every little thing our children desire. And we usually go too far. The reality of life and the cost of material possessions usually rein us in and help us to keep our heads on straight. It is good to have plans for our children, or at least be able to steer them in the right direction.

Precious Moments for Raising Christian Children

It takes a lot of work to raise children, answer their questions, and guide them wisely. We are on call 24/7. And even more work is required for Christian moms and dads to raise Christian children. We must pray very hard and ask for wisdom. I always say that it is God who raised my children, not Jeff and me. Think of the joys and sorrows that occur as our children experience school: failed tests, aced tests, pop quizzes, oral book reports, term papers, difficult teachers, and amazing teachers, not to mention the broken hearts, dating, manners, proper behaviors, bullying, and just getting along with people. Whether our children are in a private school, public school, or home schooled, there is plenty of work, communication, and discipline that must be accomplished by the parents to produce normal, healthy, young people who will mature and take the reins of society.

The Nurture and the Admonition of the Lord

What do we do when it comes to spiritual things? How will our children react to God? That answer is fairly easy. Children imitate what they see in their parents. Will we, as parents, make these choices?

- Be faithful to the Lord.
- Be involved in the work of the church.
- Teach and talk with our children constantly about God.
- Love the Lord with all our hearts, souls, minds, and strength.

Let's set the right example for our children. Then nine times out of ten our children will follow.

Some children grow up in committed, faithful Christian homes and will produce the same type of home. Others leave the faith completely. Remember, God never forces anyone to obey His gospel or love Him. We make our own choices.

Proverbs 22:6 instructs all parents, "Train up a child in the way he should go, even when he is old he will not depart from it." The good and right things we have done with our children are forever recorded in each child's memory. Perhaps they will choose to live contrary to God's law, but they will never forget the right ways they were taught. And if our children mature, leave home, and turn away from the Lord, all we can do is pray and beg God for time and opportunity: time for them to grow up and see the importance of heaven, time for them to repent, and time for us or another to be able to influence them again.

We must also grow spiritually and see God's importance. Being faithful is crucial. Going to worship and Bible study isn't all about making sure the kids get taught the Word of God. It's also about making sure we adults are spiritually fed. There is much preparation for Sundays for all involved. Do we women take the time to do some personal class preparation before we actually meet? Do we read our study material ahead of time, or do we just wing it?

The question to ask ourselves is, "What kind of Christians do our children see in us?"

Pause and Ponder

Ask your older children to evaluate your Christianity. What makes them want to be like you? What traits do they want to avoid? What behaviors are evident in them that you directly relate to your example, good or bad?

Time to Be Mighty

Steve Minor, a preacher who conducts excellent family seminars, once said, "If we are going to create a generation of mighty men and women, it won't be an accident. We have to be mighty to produce mighty!" I don't know about you, but I surely want to be mighty, and I want my children to be mighty too. Remember the saying, "A halfhearted Christian cannot follow a wholehearted Savior." Being mighty takes work, strength, determination, and guts.

Whether we are the parent or the child, there is an absolute we must consider. We all need God. This is our life. We are in the moment trying to deal with this day's evil, and the only way to survive is to talk to God. God can handle anything. I could not have made it through any phase of my life without Him. With His powerful and mighty Word guiding me, my family has survived and continues to walk with the Lord today. Has it been easy to raise two children? Absolutely not. But I surrendered myself to God long ago. And I also surrendered my daughter Jennifer and my son Jeffrey to God, as I prayed and begged God to lead them in righteousness. And that is my prayer now for my precious grandchildren.

Dr. John Trainer once said, "Children are not a distraction from more important work. They are the most important work." Who can argue with that? Girls, I want my children to make it to heaven more than anything else in the world. There is nothing more important. Am I so naïve to think that they will know about Jesus and become Christians and serve God without my influence and input? Can they get all they need spiritually on their own and without my help? No, they cannot. I still believe and will always believe that God has made women more verbal because it is Mom who teaches, Mom who guides, and Mom who points the way. My sisters, it is Mom who turns the moments into memories and teaches her children to be mighty in the Lord.

Did you know that Job provided prayers and sacrifices for his children and their relationships with God? Consider the following passage:

> When the days of feasting had completed their cycle, Job would send and consecrate them, rising up early in the morning and offering burnt offerings according to the number of them all; for Job said, "Perhaps my sons have sinned and cursed God in their hearts." Thus Job did continually (Job 1:5).

Job took sin seriously. He was the patriarchal go-between for his children and God's forgiveness. Job was in earnest about pleasing God and being forgiven. Is pleasing God and being forgiven a serious matter for us? Job looked out for his children. Shouldn't we do the same for our children? I remember my mom's remarking, "Becky, all three of you kids are in your fifties, and I am still concerned about each of you!"

Dr. James Dobson said, "If you don't introduce your children to Christ, then you will never see them again. It is the most important thing you can do." That is very blunt, isn't it? Listen to me, sisters. Teaching your children about Jesus and going to heaven is the most important thing you will ever do in this life, and it is the most important thing you must do in this life.

Where Do I Start Seeking the Precious Moments?

The first thing you can do for your child is to pray for her. Go to God continually and ask for wisdom. He will help you (James 1). Pray for God to keep a hedge of protection around your child and you (Psalm

5:12; 125:2; 139:5). Pray, pray, pray for God to help you get that child and all your children to heaven.

Take time to talk with your kids about the Father when they are in the womb and out of the womb, and don't stop until you're in the tomb! Talk and sing about God as you push them around the block in the stroller. Point out God's creation around you—the trees, grass, animals—and ask, "Who made the trees?" Say the answer repeatedly, "God did!"

Pray for and with your children. Teach them how to pray, and listen to their prayers. You are training them to communicate with the heavenly Father. Talk about the importance of prayer, and as they grow up, point out how God has answered their prayers and is constantly at work in their lives.

Whatever you do, put down that phone. It is for emergencies only. You will never have these times with your child in a stroller again, so make the most of them

It's Time to Escape the Cell

We adults are just as guilty as the kids of being "joined at the hip" to electronics. We are addicted to checking email, text messages, and social media status. Have you seen a family eating near you in a restaurant, both parents looking at their cell phones and the children looking lost, waiting for conversation? Or perhaps each family member has a cell phone and they are not communicating with one another at all. Have you seen adults texting and checking Facebook during the worship? I have. Haven't any of us realized that Satan is behind all of this?

On the Prowl

In the book and movie, *Same Kind of Different as Me*, Denver, the homeless man, makes a most remarkable statement: "Those precious to God become more important to Satan." Wiser words were never said.

When we begin our walk with the Lord as His child, Satan rushes in to halt the journey and annihilate our relationship with God. He plants landmines everywhere we go, so that we will finally just give up. Satan wants us to walk with him, not God. Most Christians love the Lord. They want to obey and please Him, but the devil wants to destroy them and anything righteous or holy. That is why he comes to church with us and walks right in that front door. He sits in Bible class and worship. He attends the showers, the fellowships, the parties—anywhere God's people gather—and he tries to get the family of God upset with the family of God. Be on the alert. Be aware.

Satan wants all our time, and he wants to keep us so busy that we have no time for spiritual pursuits of any sort. If we love that phone and all its gadgetry, then we will not talk with our family, we will not look up from the screen long enough to see what a fabulous world God has made, and we will not see the soul that God has sent for us to teach. We will miss out on everything meaningful, and that is the devil's aim.

Satan wants to reel our minds into his power and keep us addicted to the phones while little minds and eyes observe our priorities. Soon those children we love so much want a phone of their own. Then we adults see the monsters we have created. Our children will now have the power to view uncensored photos, violent games, pornography, and sexually explicit acts that we parents would never have dreamed of putting before their eyes. *Sexting* is now a cell phone reality, and teenagers can be very savvy about hiding their activities from their parents' eyes.

Oh how wise and perceptive parents must be. There is a battle going on for our souls and our children's souls. Don't be naïve, my sister. Satan is an expert when it comes to luring our hearts, minds, and children away from the Lord.

We must do everything we can to outsmart the devil. God will help us. Our children have forgotten how to play outside, so let's show them how. Let's all put down our phones and go to the lake. Let's play games together around the kitchen table. Let's go on a picnic in the backyard. Let's go to the park and walk together. Let's talk about our childhood with our kids. Let's stop and have that meaningful discussion about baptism with our children. Let's limit our time on Facebook, or better yet, do without it on some days. Let's help our kids to have healthy hearts, minds, and bodies for Jesus, and in the process, we will have these things too.

After all, how healthy is it for any of us to sit on a couch and play video games on a tiny screen all day? It is imperative that we, old and young alike, keep our minds and bodies active for the Lord's work. At the same time, we must always be aware of Satan's schemes for capturing our minds and souls. He will not stop until we die or time has ended.

Pause and Ponder

What steps will you take to fight Satan's attempts to claim you and your children? Look for a scripture to fortify you in your resolutions.

Redeem the Time

Paul's letter to the Ephesians urges Christians to redeem the time, to be wise with our precious moments.

> Therefore be careful how you walk, not as unwise men but as wise, making the most of your time, because the days are evil. So then do not be foolish, but understand what the will of the Lord is (Ephesians 5:15–17).

Were there ever any truer words? We run like crazy women, sometimes screaming banshees, trying to accomplish all the demanding tasks we encounter every day. But God tells us to make the most of the time we have because the days are evil. I once heard Paul Faulkner say, "Too many times we pay attention to the urgent things and not the important things." It never hurts to stop and assess what is really important and necessary for the day itself. Toss out the garbage and keep the important.

Before we leave Ephesians 5:15–17, let's look at the last admonition: "Understand what the will of the Lord is." What would you say the will of the Lord is?

The defining passage that comes to me is 1 Timothy 2:3–4, "This is good and acceptable in the sight of God our Savior, who desires all men to be saved and to come to the knowledge of the truth." This passage teaches us that God's will is for all men and all women to be saved.

My precious sisters, talk to your children, whether in the stroller, in the car, or on an airplane. Tell them about God, His love, and Jesus dying on the cross for them. God's will is for your children to go to heaven. Isn't that your will for them too?

Pause and Ponder

Read Deuteronomy 6:4–9. Share ways to talk to children about God. Discuss effective methods.

This Old Testament teaching on raising God's children is still successful today. Let's not overlook Deuteronomy 6:5–6. God first commands us parents—yes, it is an order!—to write His words on our own hearts first. If we parents do not, then how will our children learn to love God and the importance of going to heaven? How will they know the significance of our mighty Savior Jesus and an old rugged cross? The responsibility does not fall to their school or the church or the youth minister. It's on the shoulders of Christian parents to instruct these children we love with all our heart about the God who loves them with all His heart. If we parents don't know the Lord, neither will our children.

Someone has said, "If we don't teach our children to love Jesus, the world will teach them not to." Our children are growing up fast, and moments are precious and fleeting. Every minute counts when it comes to helping our kids cultivate their relationship with the Father.

Sunday Is His Day, Not Our Day

Start by being faithful to the Lord, to all the services of the church. Regular church attendance provides repetitive opportunities for instructing our offspring. Begin with sharing the importance of the first day of the week, the Lord's Day, not our day. Jesus arose from the dead on Sunday, the first day of the week. The church was established on the Lord's Day. Let's show our children the love that motivates us to attend every function possible. If you are a Sunday Christian only, chances are that your child will be that too, or completely drop out.

Question: What if my husband will not come to church services with me?

Answer: Then you go alone and take your children. If you have to be the strong one, then be it. Let them see your love and commitment to God take top priority. You set the example.

Being unfaithful in worship is nothing new. It's as old as the early church. God admonished in Hebrews 10:25, "Not forsaking our own assembling together, as is the habit of some, but encouraging one another; and all the more as you see the day drawing near."

Sing Bible songs in the car with the kids. We always played Bible games in the car as we rode to church. Growing up in the Fowler home, only a cappella music was allowed on Sunday morning as we prepared our minds to worship God. And the only television program we could watch was *Herald of Truth* with Batsell Barrett Baxter. Today we watch *In Search of the Lord's Way* with Phil Sanders and listen to spiritual a cappella songs.

Question: What do I do if my children do not want to play Bible games with me?

Answer: Play the Bible games anyway. I can speak about this personally because our son Jeffrey, who is now a preacher, sat in the back seat and complained and groaned. At age five, he was the prophet of doom. He was the "negative Nellie" during our Sunday journeys. I would hear this little voice from the back seat complainingly say, "I don't want to play these games."

That was my cue. "Okay, you can't play." Reverse psychology works.

Turning to my husband, I would say, "Jeff you are left handed. Did you know that there was a wonderful and mighty left-handed warrior named Ehud?"

"Really, Becky? Tell me more." (I love that man!)

I would tell a little about Ehud, and then I would launch into the next fascinating story from the Old Testament.

"Jeff, did you know that there is a man in the Old Testament whose nurse dropped him when he was a baby? Jennifer, did you know he was crippled forever?" It never failed. A small voice piped up from the back seat.

My son: "How did it happen, Mama?"

Me: "I thought you weren't playing, Jeffrey."

My son: "I want to play now. How did she drop him, Mama?"

Me: "Well, she was running and escaping from someone who was trying to kill him. She fell, and he was crippled the rest of his life. You won't believe what his name was—I bet you can't say it!"

My son: "Yes, I can. What was it?"

Me: "Mephibosheth. Spell it. M-e-p-h-i-b-o-s-h-e-t-h. Mephibosheth. He was Jonathan's son and David took care of him all his life."

My son: "Mephibosheth."

Never, never let your children stop you from teaching God's Word. Don't let them win. Remember, they are just kids and as immature as "all get out," as we say in the Southwest. You are the one in charge. You are the mama, and souls are at stake. Take charge. One time a single mom that I was trying to encourage told me that she had wanted to come to church the week before, but her little girl had said, "Mama, let's don't go to church. Let's just stay in bed and snuggle." So that is what they did, and they never came to church.

As hard as it is to believe, we can even allow our own children to keep us from God and our own salvation. And if that happens, we have only ourselves to blame. Hell is eternal. There will be no way out and no relief—ever. The bottom line is this: If we love our family and if we live for Jesus, then the two must meet.

Pause and Ponder

How can you improve your family's routine on Sunday mornings?

Time for Bible Class

My sweet sisters, I realize that this chapter is long, but invest in these important thoughts about parenting. The work women do at home is a mighty work for the Lord. In many respects, raising your family is the most important work you will ever do for God. Let's think about taking our family to the house of the Lord.

Take your children to Bible class, and of course, go to Bible class yourself. Some parents drop their children off for class and then go for coffee. Don't even go there. Be where they learn and you learn. I am so thankful for Bible teachers who faithfully teach, love, and instruct our children Sundays and Wednesdays, year in and year out. The classroom setting is where we all can ask questions, look at maps, openly discuss problems, and realize that the Bible is alive.

Don't you agree that the Bible class hour is when the most biblical learning and growing occur? Certainly, we do develop in knowledge and understanding during the worship service, and the preacher's sermons have great impact and importance. But there is usually more time in a class period than in a sermon. In addition to that, our children's class periods are geared for learning with age-appropriate materials, discussion times, and hands-on resources. Most congregations provide a Bible study for all ages twice a week—Sunday and Wednesday. Appreciate and take advantage of all the opportunities at your fingertips to grow in the faith. But consider this most of all. Satan is working extra hard on Sundays and Wednesdays to keep you and me from the house of the Lord. Beware, my sisters, Satan is doing everything he possibly can to keep you away from God and His Word. Don't let Satan win!

I urge you, my young sisters with families, please, please, get your precious kids to Bible school on time. Prepare for Sunday on Saturday. Lay out clothes and shoes on Saturday night. I emphasize the shoes because Satan hides shoes and socks on Sunday mornings, so be on your toes to defeat the devil every Sunday. Trust me, Satan will do his best to make your home a war zone on Sunday mornings—kids crying, mom and dad screaming—sheer pandemonium to the point that you will say, "Oh, this is just too much. Let's just stay home!" And the score is: Satan—1; God—0.

Sunday is our day to meet God and tell Him we love Him. Arrive on time. Many families come straggling into class twenty minutes late. By that time, your children have missed much of the class, and you have too. I have not met a child yet who hated Sunday school. They all enjoy learning about God, so set your clock a little earlier Sunday morning. It can make all the difference between peace and a battlefield. Even we adults need to improve in this category.

Precious Moments Close to God

In Robert Coles' book, *The Story of Ruby Bridges*, a six-year-old girl was selected as one of four black girls to go to a white elementary school in New Orleans in 1960. Listen to this touching comment from Ruby's mother about making sure the children attended church: "We wanted them to start feeling close to Him from the very start." Was she right? I think so. Like Ruby's mother, we should also want to be wherever God is.

God gives His children of all ages a simple admonition in Ecclesiastes 5:1 when He says, "Guard your steps as you go to the house of God and draw near to listen rather than to offer the sacrifice of fools." Watch how you walk; prepare yourself as you go to God's house. Prepare your mind and be ready to worship rather than to talk flippantly. I cannot emphasize enough the value of preparing to meet God in three Persons every single time you walk into the church building.

Pause and Ponder

Read the following scriptures: Psalm 16:8; 34:18; 73:28; Jeremiah 23:23; 1 Samuel 14:36; Acts 17:26–28. What do these verses have in common? How do they help you?

Seek Times of Participation

Surely we realize that our children do not miss a beat in watching us worship. We must let them see us singing joyfully. Aren't we thankful to be God's children? We must let them see us partake of the Lord's supper in a serious manner. Aren't we deeply grateful for Jesus' death, burial, and resurrection? We must let them see us give cheerfully. Aren't we thankful for all our blessings? In watching us, they learn how to be active participants.

Show your child how to sing with the songbook. Urge him to open his little mouth and praise God. Show him how. My sisters, God has given every one of us a voice in order to praise Him, and He wants to hear it from all of us, regardless of age or voice quality. The human voice is the body's instrument from God. Surely one valid reason for not using mechanical instruments in worship is because God expects us to use what He has already given us—our own voices.

We decide how much we want to use our voices in worship. We may give God a little, or we may give Him all we have. Some do not sing at all. Some sing very softly because they are embarrassed or don't like their voice. And some folks just don't like to sing. But hear me out on this. Whether we like it or not, God has told us to sing.

Ephesians 5:19–20 "Speaking to one another in psalms and hymns and spiritual songs, singing and making melody with your heart to the Lord; always giving thanks for all things in the name of our Lord Jesus Christ to God, even the Father."

I have always loved to sing. Perhaps that is because my parents loved to sing, and they taught us to sing. It's contagious. We sang everywhere we went, and we were frequently in the car. And rest assured, I was never allowed to sit on a pew and not lift up my voice to God.

What other way can we participate in worship? By using our Bibles. And be sure that your children have a Bible with them on Sundays. If you don't bring a Bible, why should they? If it's not important to you to look up passages during the service, your children will not see the Bible's importance. Why should they think any differently?

As they learn to read, help them find the verses while the preacher quotes them. When a prayer is offered, hold your child's hand and bow your head. Show reverence to the Father.

Children love to put money in the collection plate, so make sure they participate in giving. It's smart to wait until immediately before the plate is passed to hand children money, or you might find yourself embarrassed and crawling under your pew to retrieve their coins or bills. There will be times you will have to shake their sweet little clenched fists and quietly say with gritted teeth, "I said to drop it!"

Get a notebook and take notes together. Let them observe the importance of God's Word to you. Our congregation provides "Eutychus and You" papers. Any child can pick up one of those brightly colored sheets in the foyer and take notes on the sermon. If they take notes and hand them to our preacher's wife, they are rewarded with a piece of candy. Believe me, that little piece of candy motivates them to listen. Even the children who cannot write will sit up and listen and draw a picture of what they think the sermon is about.

Don't you think that we all can improve our worship? Taking notes, finding the Bible passages, singing joyfully, praying reverently, and giving cheerfully will make us grow. Worship is important and our lively participation results in joy and happiness. We leave the church building feeling good, peaceful, and eager to do more for the Lord. Rather than whining, "Well, I certainly didn't get anything out of that service," we exclaim, "Wow, our worship today was truly moving and wonderful!" Why? Because we participated. We put ourselves into it.

My parents always knew what was happening on that family pew, and one of their children not singing, passing notes, not bowing their head to pray, or talking and misbehaving was instantly handled. This was Sunday. This was worship to God. We were to give our best. That is training your children to worship and respect God.

Pause and Ponder

Relate some worship experiences you have had or seen. Be prepared to laugh a lot. It's okay, I believe God has a marvelous sense of humor.

Time to Be All You Can Be as Parents

You can bet that Joshua took child-raising to another level simply because he knew the importance of serving God. All parents need these words written in their hearts: "But as for me and my house, we will serve the Lord" (Joshua 24:15).

What can be more wonderful than being a Christian and having Christian parents? I realize that not every home has two parents who are believers that place God at the helm of their Christian family. I am forever indebted to my precious parents who took child raising seriously. I am grateful to my Lord for their love and example. I always knew that God was number one with them, and then came us kids. It is one thing to tell a child how to live, and it is another thing to live it in front of a child.

How easy it is to verbally knock today's youth, their manners and their behavior. We can criticize them until we are blue in the face and condemn them for their attitudes. Generations have done it for years. However, we often aim our fault findings in the wrong direction. These young people are just doing what comes naturally because that is what they have been permitted to do all along. They have not been taught differently. The real problem here is the parents.

Moments Turn to Years–Have Fun with Kids

My mom always took me with her to the store. And all we did was talk, talk, talk. She was using her busy moments to be with me. Let's allow our children to express their opinions peacefully while we do the same. Listen, laugh with them, tell jokes together, and be silly. The more we communicate, the stronger our relationships will be. The stronger the bonds between us and our children, the more they trust us and bring us their problems and concerns. That is what all parents want. Be open and honest with them, even telling them that you identify with them. Apologize when necessary, and always assure them of your love for them.

Families must have fun together. Plan a yearly vacation and make memories. You will laugh through the years when your child says, "Hey, Mom, do you remember the time we went to. . . . " You will even laugh at the bad memories of vacations. The point is that they remember too.

Where Did Everybody Go?

I hear this question a lot: "Where are our young people? We are losing them. They're gone, you know." I have heard that for years.

I have some questions: "Where are our grownups? Where are the adults? Where are the senior citizens?"

We are losing them just as fast as our youth, but do you ever hear anything about them? No. Look around you. Observe your congregation. Where are the new converts? Are they coming to the services a year after their conversion? Where are the adults? Are they faithful? Not as many as you would think and hope. Where are the families? Like Elvis, they all have left the building.

God has taken a back seat in the minivan headed for the ball field, the mall, and birthday parties. I honestly believe that in some places if it were announced on Sunday morning that Jesus would be at the Sunday evening service, some Christians would not show up. Not show up to meet Jesus? Oh, yes. Folks who are not faithful to gather with our God-given family have already chosen not to meet Jesus anyway.

Check out the attendance board. Do only a handful of the faithful return on Sunday night and Wednesday night? It's true that many young people are absent from the church services, but so are the older people. Too many folks don't have time for God.

Satan's Clever Tool

Let's take this a step further and ask more questions. How many Christians know what the Bible says? How many can quote five scriptures? What about being in the Word? Do an anonymous survey in your congregation asking, "Are you a daily Bible reader? Do you pray at least once a day? Are you like Daniel who stopped three times a day, got on his knees, and prayed to God?" Ask the adults to name the twelve tribes of Israel. Ask Bible questions such as: Who was the mother of Ishmael? Can you name Isaac and Rebekah's sons? Who were the women who bore the twelve sons of Jacob? Who were the twelve apostles? What was the Babylonian captivity all about? Can you name the sixty-six books of the Bible?

I know of a congregation that gave the adult classes a quiz occasionally which included the question asking if Jesus were a Jew or a Gentile. A certain percentage of that class flunked it every time.

It breaks my heart to tell you that the average Christian cannot answer these questions. Why not? Why aren't these facts written on the hearts of God's children? Because often they do not care enough to learn them. Because these facts are not special enough for Christians to seek the precious moments to memorize. Because many think the

Bible is not important, which really means whatever God has told us is not important either.

It takes work, time, and sacrifice to learn and grow in the knowledge of God, and we are selfish children, actually called "children of wrath" in Scripture (Ephesians 2:3). How many parents teach biblical concepts to their children? How many families sing Bible songs and play Bible games?

What saddens me even more is to know that my brothers and sisters do not know the Father, the one who made us, guides us, and saves us from eternal hell. Oh yes, many Christians desire to be saved by the Father. They run to Him in emergencies, but they don't want to invest time it takes to learn Him. Someone has said, "Many Christians grow up in church but never grow in Christ. They know hymns, but they don't know Him."

Gregory Alan Tidwell once admonished the Lads to Leaders/Leaderettes,

> What does it profit our children if they should letter in four sports, be accepted into the most prestigious college, and rise to the top of a lucrative profession, but in the process lose their souls?

Oh, my sisters, please remember this: Satan's cleverest tool is man's ignorance of God's Word. Satan will do everything in his bag of tricks to keep you and me from opening the Bible or reading it, much less studying it and maturing into what God wants us to be. When it comes to salvation, our final destination is heaven or hell. Ignorance is not bliss. As parents, we need to "wake up and smell the coffee" when it comes to our role as our children's guide to the Father. "Train up a child in the way he should go, even when he is old, he will not depart from it" (Proverbs 22:6).

God Speaks

Hosea 4:6 may have been written 2,500 years ago, but this powerhouse verse is still relevant. "My people are destroyed for lack of knowledge." God said it.

How do we prevent this? How do we get knowledge? Clearly, we need to get back to the Bible. The Bible is our handbook, atlas, guidebook, and love letter all rolled up into one unequaled volume. It has all the answers we will ever need.

Pause and Ponder

What does the Father want His children to do with their Christian lives? Read the following passages for your answer: Colossians 3:16; 2 Peter 3:17–18.

What will it take for us to open the Bible and learn from it? Do we take God and His merciful grace for granted? Why isn't God more important to us? It's because we have put ourselves on the throne that we worship the most. It's all about us. Someone wisely has said, "If you're not hungry for God, you may be too full of yourself."

Here's an article I clipped from our local paper some time back. It speaks volumes.

DIRECTION FOR THE FUTURE

A young college student, who did not grow up attending church, once asked to meet with me for lunch. He was pursuing a degree in English literature and now, he lamented, he had discovered that the great English classics are filled with references to the Bible, stories he had never learned.

How will the next generation learn the stories that inform human behavior, faith, and character? Most children do not attend church and parents themselves often lack knowledge of the Bible. They neither read the stories nor tell them to their children. Public schools are not allowed to teach them.

Who will tell the stories of Adam and Eve, Cain and Abel, Noah and the flood, Abraham, Isaac and Jacob, Joseph, Moses and the Exodus, Ruth and Boaz, David, Elijah, Jonah, and Jesus' life, death, and resurrection? The uncertainty about our nation and the world may be due to the fact that we are losing the stories of our heritage that give direction for the future."

The Bible says, "I will utter hidden things, things from of old, things we have heard and known, things our ancestors have told us. We will not hide them from their descendants. We will tell the next generation the praiseworthy deeds of the Lord, His power, and the wonders He has done . . . so the next generation would know them, even the children yet to be born, and they in turn would tell their children. Then they would put their trust in God and would not forget His deeds but would keep His commands" (Psalm 78:2–7).[40]

Commitment to Training

Once our family visited a congregation with a packed auditorium. A lady with three boys sat in front of us. Two of the boys were fourth graders and the other one was probably in the seventh grade. The two younger boys promptly got down on the floor and played with games and puzzles during the entire service, while the older one, sitting next to his mother, entertained himself with a Rubik's cube. When the two boys got on the floor, she told them in a loud voice so that all could hear: "Now remember, boys, when you get into the fifth grade you can't play on the floor anymore." They never looked at her or acknowledged her. To add more to this scene, a child behind us had a video game with screen. Voices and music were constantly going throughout the worship.

Girls, this is not training your children to *love God*. This is training your children to *tune out God* with devices, toys, and games. What do we expect, since the kids see adults texting and checking emails instead of worshiping? Many of them want us to think they are using the Bible app on their phone. What are we thinking? The truth is, we are not thinking. We are allowing Satan to take the wheel and steer our lives right into absolute chaos.

It's a choice of the parents whether or not to teach Jesus. It takes energy to deal with obstinate children who refuse to obey; it's easier to give in and let them have their own way. It takes strength to dig our heels in and lay down the laws of home and family.

Dads have to be strong too. Paul urged them, "Fathers, do not provoke your children to anger, but bring them up in the discipline and instruction of the Lord" (Ephesians 6:4). How crucial it is for us to remember that our children are watching us, and they will imitate what they see.

If we do not wake up and make it our mission to get our kids to heaven, we most likely will experience the agony of not only seeing our children with miserable shredded lives but also of seeing their lost souls. And that is utter heartbreak, because we contributed to our own children's downfall.

Precious Parents

Many a young mom has come to me with tears in her eyes, feeling inadequate because she had no time to work for the Lord. Due to staying home with her children, she was not always able to visit the sick, attend a funeral, or be a part of the ladies' prayer group. She felt that she was shirking her Christian duties.

Please, please, if this is you, my sister, stop right there. Please hear me on this: Your children *are* your work. You will have time when they are gone to do more tasks for the Lord. There is not a more worthy work right now than raising your children in the "nurture and admonition of the Lord." Your home is their world where they are fed physically, mentally, and spiritually. You are their nurturer, and there is no higher calling than being called "Mama," except being called "Christian."

> The home is a battleground for the soul. Failing the tests of home lays the foundation for a delinquent life. It is not an exaggeration to

affirm that a number of parents fail the test of spiritual parenthood. Husbands and fathers fail the headship test. Apart from their personal salvation, the greatest needs of wives, mothers, and children are Christian husbands and fathers with whom their hearts can safely rest because they know those men are going to lead their homes in spiritual truths and concerns.

They need men of such spiritual quality and headship strength as Joshua who can speak for their families and say, "As for me and my house, we will serve the Lord" (Joshua 24:15).[41]

I was raised in an unusual family. I do believe most missionary children are raised the way I was. Our precious family of five talked about heaven all the time. My parents were focused on salvation, and that made a huge and lasting impression on us kids. If a family is ever going to see the importance of eternity with the Lord, then someone needs to start the conversation. And in my book, that needs to be the parents. My mom's favorite song was "When We All Get to Heaven," and my dad always said it was because "Lea wants to take everybody she meets to heaven with her."

I speak from experience when I say that when parents love the Lord and live to save others, the family knows about eternity.

Everybody Wants to Go to Heaven

Let's be honest: Everybody wants to go to heaven, but the reality is that not all will obey God's rules and make it there. Everybody wants to go to heaven where God is, but they don't want to go to church where God is. Someone once said, "So, you don't want to go to His house on earth, yet you expect to live in His mansion forever." Heaven is a prepared place for a prepared people. Getting to heaven will not be an accident.

I was looking through my mom's lessons several years ago, and I found this quote from an unknown author: "If everyone could just get a glimpse of either heaven or hell, the church buildings would be full." Oh, yes. The church buildings would be packed.

A Precious Gift

Don't you think we could talk about our children and our family for forty days and forty nights? This has been a strong chapter for many reasons. But I think the main reason we must take this child raising so seriously is that we will never, never get this opportunity again. Our children will be young only once, and we are in charge of guiding their steps. This is a one-shot deal. We may not even live to see our grandchildren, so our family time is dear. This is it. Parents have a child for about eighteen years and then she is off on her own, pursuing college, a career, or marriage. We know how things changed when we left home, so labor diligently during the fleeting moments you have with this precious soul.

Solomon was inspired to say, "Behold, children are a gift of the LORD, the fruit of the womb is a reward" (Psalm 127:3). That beautiful child that you carried, bore, rocked, taught, and raised truly is a gift from our precious Father who chose you to be Mama to her. Hopefully, that child will be a great reward.

Never Stop Praying

As we close these thoughts on family, I want to say something from my heart to yours. Never cease praying (1 Thessalonians 5:17). Prayer is our lifeline to our merciful Father. I heard a wonderful preacher at a lectureship talking about prayer. He was very honest as he revealed something extremely personal in his family. When his son was young, the preacher prayed that God would protect him and watch over him—the things we parents certainly have prayed. But his son grew and he left the Lord. "As a result," the preacher said, "I don't pray that prayer anymore. Now I pray that God will do whatever has to be done to bring my son back to Him."

Girls, we do not know or cannot foretell what our children will do. We pray that they will love the Lord and serve Him all of their days. But if they do not, we will never stop praying like Jesus did, "Lord, not

My will, but Your will be done on earth as it is in heaven." We will continue to be faithful even if our children are not. We will not look back. Please keep in mind that at the end of the day, salvation is between us and God, and all we can do is save ourselves.

MOMENTS IN PRAYER

Oh, Lord, please bless us all, the moms and the dads and the children we love. When You gave us Jesus, You gave us the gift of all gifts. Our children are Your children. We give them back to You the way it would please You the most. Like Hannah, we have taught them that they belong to You. Help us, Lord, to find the time to do all we can to get them to heaven. O Lord, help us to be strong. We love You, Lord. In Jesus' name, Amen.

Back Home

If I had the power to turn back the clock,
Go back to that house at the end of the block.
The house that was home when I was a kid,
I know that I'd love it more now than I did.

If I could be back there at my mother's knee,
And hear once again, the things she told me.
I'd listen as I never listened before,
For she knew so well just what life had in store.

And all the advice my dad used to give,
His voice I'll remember as long as I live.
But it didn't seem really important then,
What I'd give to live it all over again.

And what I'd give for the chance I once had,
To do so much more for my mom and dad.
To give them more joy and little less pain,
A little more sunshine—a little less rain.

But the years roll on and we cannot go back,
Whether we were born in a mansion or a shack.
But we can start right now in the hour that's here,
To do something more for the ones I hold dear.

And since time in its flight is traveling so fast,
Let's not spend it regretting that which is past.
But let's make tomorrow a happier day,
By doing my "good unto others"—today.

—Author Unknown[42]

Moments in Song

"A Wonderful Savior" and "God's Family"

KEEP SEEKING

1. Read Joshua 24:15. What house was Joshua talking about?
2. How important is it for you and your family to read the Bible and pray?
3. How could your family improve in its Bible knowledge?

66 Timely Quotes 99

"A lack of church programs and entertainment is not why our youth are leaving the church. Our youth have no relationship with Jesus and that begins at home. Until we focus on fixing that, all the entertainment in the world won't keep them."

—Facebook

"I don't believe we lose young people because of what churches do. I believe we lose our young people because of what parents do."

—Jerry Elder, Facebook

"If we do not answer our children's questions about creation, evolution will answer every single one of them."

—Tour guide, at a visit to the Creation Museum

"Women can give up their jobs as clerks, engineers, doctors, and other people will step in, and the world will go as smoothly as before. Not so with mothering. When we leave this job, the world does not go on as before. It falters and begins to lose its way."

—Unknown

"What you leave behind is not what is engraved in stone monuments, but what is woven into the lives of others."

—Pericles

"I Just Want to Help"

I can still see her in my mind, a young woman about thirty years old. I cannot even tell you her name, but her long dark hair and long dangling earrings, those I remember. I only saw her about half a dozen times. I was about fifteen when she first walked into the church building in Concord, New Hampshire, in the 1960s.

What impressed me most was her nonstop weeping. She would cry through the worship, and afterwards I would see her in a corner with Mom's arms around her. Mom would be listening, nodding her head, and speaking quietly with her. This woman would disappear for several months and then reappear to worship with us. Again, she was always weeping.

One Sunday she attended services and as usual, collapsed into my mother's arms after the closing prayer. I knew that something was very seriously wrong in her life, but I did not know what it was. She obviously trusted my mother enough to spill her heart out and reveal her heavy sorrow.

Finally, I asked, "Mom, what is wrong with that lady at church who cries all the time?"

And my precious mom looked at me and said sadly, "Becky, that woman had an abortion, and she cannot get over it."

I understood. Abortion is so sad and so final, and this one occurred long before *Roe v. Wade*. It was an illegal abortion. Oh, the heartbreak and the never-ending guilt that accompanies that act.

I do not know any other details about this woman. She simply dropped out of sight. I think of her as the crying woman who was absolutely heartbroken.

Second Memory

Perhaps you have read about my love for Gander Brook Christian Camp in Maine. I thank God for good Christian camps and for godly men and women who spend their summers diligently working to provide a spiritual surrounding for kids from various backgrounds. I'm filled with wonderful memories of attending that camp, summer after summer.

At the end of the summer camping sessions, three retreats follow on successive weekends. First, the ladies' retreat; then the men's retreat; finally a singles' retreat.

When I go to the ladies' retreat, it seems like a piece of heaven. The sisters' singing, the deep spiritual lessons, and the laughter and the tears all collide to make that event like none other. Frankly, the most outstanding thing about these women is their eagerness to learn more about God. My mom always made the claim, "There is no place like Gander Brook!" And she was right.

When I went with Mom, one thing happened repeatedly. I would lose Mom. I would turn around from a chat, and Mom would be gone. Instantly. I'd scan the lodge, the dining room, the pavilion, or the grassy paths around the camp and usually find her in one of these places.

Mom was never alone in one of these spots. Some sister needed her advice. I see her in my mind, walking slowly across a grassy knoll arm in arm with a sister, deep in conversation. Sometimes she was in a corner of the pavilion, listening intently and carefully choosing her words as she replied to a sister's dilemma.

Once I was just plain nosy, so I decided to walk closer and eavesdrop. I was hoping she was saying her farewells. As I drew nearer and nearer to their conversation, I heard Mom say, "Well, honey, I am just trying to help."

My sisters, that is an important comment to anyone, isn't it? "I am just trying to help." What would the Lord have us do? Help. Teach. And above all, love, and help some more.

Mom was a Barnabas. She knew how to encourage Christians, from the weakest to the strongest. She opened her arms and heart and loved people. She encouraged the new converts in leading singing, prayers, and scripture reading. The men in the congregation loved her and called her "Mama." Both men and women found acceptance, trust, and comfort with Mom. She was their confidant.

Mom was also "Mama" to a whole lot of women. She told me time and again that I had to learn to share her, because she had many daughters. I treasure the memory of Mom, always talking, helping, and loving other women, wherever she was. You see, Mama set the example for me. She taught me how to listen, to love, and to help.

Women are the best comforters. I think it is due to the nurturing instinct God gave us. I do believe men try to help too. When a woman in a congregation goes through a horrible crisis, a group of women gather around her. Perhaps a few men offer help, but several women are there, embracing the victim and trying to comfort her, some of them even for many months.

On numerous occasions after a class or retreat lesson, a sister has privately come to me and honestly implored,

"Becky, please pray for me. I am an alcoholic."

"Becky, please pray for me. Our daughter has run away from home."

"Becky, please pray for me. My husband has told me he wants a divorce. He just doesn't want to be married anymore."

"Becky, please pray for me. My son is in prison."

"Becky, please pray for me. My husband is addicted to pornography."

"Becky, please pray for me. Our daughter is a lesbian."

My sisters, no one has a perfect life or husband or family. And the church is not perfect either. Only Jesus is perfect. We must not be shocked by all the addictions and problems Satan rains down upon us. Christians are as susceptible to trials as anybody. In fact, I believe Satan works harder on Christians than on the worldly.

This I do know: God can forgive anything, and everybody needs a Barnabas. We need someone who will say, "Honey, I am just trying to help."

12

She Has Done What She Could

W
e have come a long way, my sisters. We have built our house, filled its rooms with the precious treasures from God, and cleaned it through and through. We have constructed a memory porch in our brains, raised a family, and encountered Jesus. We have even taken off our shoes. But there are still precious moments to share before we part. One is the story of two people and how they treated God.

A Tale of Two Hearts

Pack up your minds and go on a time trip with me. Let's go back about thirty-eight hundred years to a tent in Palestine and consider a young man named Esau, twin brother of Jacob. Born to Isaac and Rebekah, Esau was the older son—the one with all the rights. God had even told a questioning pregnant Rebekah, "Two nations are in your womb; and two peoples will be separated from your body; and one people shall be stronger than the other; and the older shall serve the younger" (Genesis 25:23).

Of course, our omniscient God knew the hearts of Esau and Jacob. He was well aware of their true desires and natures, and their conflict began in the womb. God had already foreseen that Jacob would father the twelve tribes of Israel and someday be renamed Israel. No longer would Jacob be called the heel grabber, supplanter, or layer of snares that he once was, but he would have the unparalleled blessing to be in the direct lineage of the Savior of the world, Jesus Christ.

But what about Esau? What is the profound lesson hidden in the Scriptures to be discovered about him? It is found in the Old Testament and in the New Testament—Genesis 25 and Hebrews 12. Let's go back to the first account of the birthright: an unspiritual hungry hunter and a manipulating younger brother.

> When Jacob had cooked stew, Esau came in from the field and he was famished; and Esau said to Jacob, "Please let me have a swallow of that red stuff there, for I am famished." Therefore his name was called Edom [Red]. But Jacob said, "First sell me your birthright." Esau said, "Behold, I am about to die; so of what use then is the birthright to me?" And Jacob said, "First swear to me"; so he swore to him, and sold his birthright to Jacob. Then Jacob gave Esau bread and lentil stew; and he ate and drank, and rose and went on his way. Thus Esau despised his birthright (Genesis 25:29–34).

Mothers know how different each child can be. It certainly was true of Rebekah's children. Even though they were twins, Jacob and Esau were completely opposite in natures and personalities. One was an outdoors man, hunting and killing game. Nothing wrong with that. The other was an indoors man, perhaps bookish, inquisitive, and a "foodie." Nothing wrong with that either.

But when a starving Esau came back from hunting one day and smelled what Jacob was cooking, their lives were forever altered. Esau asked for a bowl of beans, and Jacob quickly asked for Esau's birthright. The birthright was an honor for the oldest son and the promise of a double-portion inheritance. Esau should have rejected Jacob's request instantly, but he didn't.

"How could Esau turn that birthright over?" we ask. Did Esau really think he was going die of hunger? Or was it perhaps that his father Isaac was so wealthy and generous that money wasn't even an object for the oldest? Or is there more to this story? Remember, neither parent was involved in this scene in the tent's kitchen.

We simply have these words from the mouth of God: "Thus Esau despised his birthright." He hated his rights as the firstborn son? No, let's look at the Hebrew word for *despise* here. It is *bazah*, and it means "to have contempt for something or someone, to disesteem, to not value something." Esau had no regard for the covenant that was spoken between God and Abraham and handed down to Isaac to teach his own sons concerning rights, inheritance, promises. Esau was selfish, putting his stomach before his heritage.

Pause and Ponder

Look up at least three different versions and their renderings of Genesis 25:34. Write the translations for the phrase "despised his birthright." How are we sometimes guilty of that offense?

I am always amazed at how God brings an Old Testament character into the New Testament to teach a principle. We see God repeating this practice in the book of Hebrews. There the writer speaks with great intensity and emphasis about the better covenant, living for Jesus, the church, running the Christian race, and not returning to Judaism. Then he refers to Esau.

> See to it that no one comes short of the grace of God; that no root of bitterness springing up causes trouble, and by it many be defiled; that there be no immoral or godless person like Esau, who sold his own birthright for a single meal. For you know that even afterwards, when he desired to inherit the blessing, he was rejected, for he found no place for repentance, though he sought for it with tears (Hebrews 12:15–17).

What an amazing and profound passage! Take your time and read it again. Verse 16 describes Esau as immoral and godless. That gives us a slant on Esau not previously seen. Have we ever thought about Esau in those terms, without God and without morals? Would we like for God to use those words to describe us?

Let's look carefully at what Burton Coffman has to say about this all-important birthright.

> Relying solely upon the Genesis account of Esau and the ordinary implications of the word *profane,* it would appear to be a safe speculation that Esau was both profane and an adulterer, each sin being inherent in the other. . . . A profane person is the opposite of a holy person.
>
> Esau . . . sold his birthright. This remarkable incident . . . involving the transfer of the birthright for the smallest considerations, only a pot of lentils, prompts a look at just what the birthright entailed. It was the most extensive right that could change hands on the basis of heredity and included (1) the right of primogeniture, that is, the right of the firstborn to receive a double portion of his father's earthly possessions. Under it, Esau would have been the head of Isaac's house, and in a sense the ruler of his brethren. (2) The right to convey the blessing to his own posterity. (3) The right of the priesthood, making its possessor the patriarchal religious leader of his people. (4) The right of custodianship of the sacred promises regarding Messiah and the promised "seed" of Abraham. It seems nearly unbelievable that any man with any regard at all for sacred and holy things should have despised them all and bartered them away for a bowl of beans. . . . Esau had become such a man as could not be the head of the tribes of Israel, nor stand in the forefront of the people as a priest of God. Whether or not Isaac, at the time it happened, knew that God's hand was in Jacob's receiving the blessing, he certainly knew it by the time mentioned here when Esau sought earnestly to change the matter; thus it is said that Esau found no place for a change in the mind of his father.[43]

Esau sold out. Esau despised, had contempt, and hated his birthright. Thus, Esau despised, had contempt, and hated the very thing that would have blessed him his entire life—God and His law. Esau obviously played by his own rules and had complete contempt for godly things. Genesis 36 even tells of Esau's marrying Canaanite women, a decision that displeased his parents and God. And when God came calling, it was Jacob who inherited all the blessings. Esau was completely overlooked. Esau was not the kind of man needed to hold twelve families together, a nation known as Israel, the children of God. This promised nation would be larger than the stars of heaven or sand on the seashore. Esau was in line for huge blessings from the Biggest Giver, but received nothing. Why? He had no time, no regard, and no respect for God. He had nothing but contempt for His heavenly Father.

When we carefully consider a Bible character, we must realize that God is omniscient. He knows our hearts. Sometimes we are too quick to judge an account from the Bible, and say something like, "Well, the Lord sure acted harshly there." We must remember that God sees the entire picture, even that particular person's heart, and we do not.

Pause and Ponder

Find the common thread in these verses: 1 Samuel 16:7; Job 34:21; Psalm 33:13; 44:21

Esau Was All about Esau

What a profound, sad account of two brothers, twins raised by the same parents, yet with different hearts for God. I often wonder what kind of parents Isaac and Rebekah were and if they found the time for God and godly teaching. I wonder too if Rebekah or Isaac had told Esau of Rebekah's conversation with the Lord before the twins were born. If so, that could explain some of Esau's contempt for God.

Today's Esau

Haven't we seen this in families too? Sometimes a child of Christian parents leaves the faith, despises God's laws, and becomes godless while his siblings remain faithful to God's Word. How does that happen? That's simple. God never forces anyone to love Him or His commandments. He gives us all the freedom of choice, and we decide on our own whom we will serve. Esau made his own decisions, and finding time for God, seeking spiritual matters, or pursuing morality was not on his list of priorities. Esau was all about Esau.

Jason Jackson had this to say about Esau:

> Esau was, in this first respect, like many people today. They don't have a burning desire to be in fellowship with Jesus Christ, nor do they have a passion about living with the Father throughout eternity, singing his praises. But one thing is sure: they don't want to go to hell. Such is the extent of their shallow spirituality. Esau had a minimal level of interest in the patriarchal promises, but it was certainly not enough.
>
> Second, although Esau knew the seriousness of the inheritance, he traded instant gratification for the patriarchal birthright, and he subsequently lost the blessing. It was not a split-second, off-the-cuff, weak-moment mistake. He was a profane man, the Hebrews writer says, and lived with a low view of the sacred promises of God. Thus, he was ripe for the temptation to "sell his birthright."
>
> Third, when the blessing was bestowed on his brother in patriarchal fashion, it was unalterable. Here is the point for the Christian. Esau lived on the fringe of spiritual concern. He lost out on the blessing, and it was unchangeable. If we live for the moment, with a light appreciation for the Christian inheritance and the blood that bought it, we can lose our opportunity, and there is no second chance. There is no other way, no use for tears, no chance for repentance after death or the Judgment (Hebrews 9:27).[44]

In her Bible, written beside "Esau despised his birthright" in Genesis 25:34, my precious mom wrote, "God will not give blessings to those who will despise them."

Pause and Ponder

Discuss Esau's character in light of Philippians 3:19.

The Rest of the Esau-Jacob Story

Before we leave this engrossing account of two brothers and the lost inheritance, let's not forget that the two brothers do meet again after a twenty-year hiatus. What happens? When the two brothers see one another, they embrace, and there is love and peace between them again. Read Genesis 33 and see that Jacob mentions the name of God, His blessings, and His graciousness. Perhaps Esau also gave God credit, but there is no record of it. And let us not forget that the Edomites, the offspring of Esau, were Israel's continual enemy in the Old Testament.

Our Sister Mary's Heart

Now let's pack another suitcase and go for another trip in New Testament times. Let's stop in Bethany because our sweet sister Mary lives there. All four Gospel accounts reveal something about this good woman whose sister was Martha, her brother was Lazarus, and her father most likely was Simon the leper.

> Now as they were traveling along, He entered a village; and a woman named Martha welcomed Him into her home. She had a sister called Mary, who was seated at the Lord's feet, listening to His word (Luke 10:38–39).

Older sister Martha was busy in the kitchen with her pots and pans and getting supper ready while little sister Mary was seated at Jesus' feet, learning and listening. We women understand the scene and the vexed nature of Martha, needing Mary's right hand to help prepare food for at least twelve hungry men. But we also understand Mary's longing to sit and listen to the profound teaching of the Savior. She had an opportunity we all desire—to sit and listen to Jesus. What was more important to her? Nothing. How did Jesus honor Mary on this occasion? He said, "She has chosen the good part" (Luke 10:42).

We see three scenes of this Mary: seated at Jesus feet; standing at Lazarus' resurrection, and sharing the last few days of Jesus' life.

Anointing in Bethany

Three of the four Gospels tell of an event with Mary at Simon the leper's house in Bethany. Burton Coffman sheds a great light concerning this Simon:

> Simon the leper refers to a Simon who had been cured of leprosy, not to one who was at that time stricken with that disease. Since Christ alone was able to cure that malady, this means that Christ had healed Simon, and probably out of gratitude, Simon held this dinner in his home for Jesus.[45]

Girls, let's make sure that we completely understand that the Gospel accounts of Mary's anointing Jesus with her expensive perfume is not the same account that Luke records in Luke 7 at the home of a Pharisee named Simon. Here a woman anointed Jesus with perfume too. Simon was a very common name, and this event happened earlier in Jesus ministry at a home in Galilee, not Bethany.

Pause and Ponder

Read each account of Mary's anointing Jesus at Bethany: Matthew 26:6–13; Mark 14:3–9; John 12:1–8. Take a piece of paper and draw three columns, labeling them Matthew, Mark, and John. Compare and contrast the accounts.

If you and I could just be in that room in Bethany for a moment, what would we see? Let's consider some of the facts the Bible gives us.

1. John names this woman as Mary.

2. Matthew and Mark both say that Jesus remarks, "She has done a good deed."

3. All three accounts have Jesus defending her and rebuking the apostles.

4. Matthew and Mark record that Mary broke the box and poured the perfume on Jesus' head while John records that Mary anointed the feet of Jesus and wiped his feet with her hair. Anointing His head showed honor; anointing His feet showed devotion.

5. Matthew and Mark say that some of the disciples disapprove of Mary's wasting the perfume, while John records that it is Judas, the thief, who complains about the cost of the perfume.

6. Mark and John record that the perfume was spikenard, a precious perfume extracted from plants grown in the high elevations of the Himalayas. It also is mentioned in Song of Solomon 1:12; and 4:13–14.

7. Matthew and Mark record that Jesus said, "Wherever the gospel is preached in the whole word, what this woman has done will also be spoken of in memory of her."

Three Outstanding Moments

When I travel in my mind to this home in Bethany, three outstanding moments make me pause, think, and imagine.

1. *Service and the senses.* "Mary then took a pound of very costly perfume of pure nard, and anointed the feet of Jesus and wiped His feet with her hair; and the house was filled with the fragrance of the perfume" (John 12:3). Imagine how the fragrance was floating up and filling

the house, and how for one moment everyone in that room smelled the loveliness of perfume and saw the loveliness of this woman. Yes, Mary was preparing Jesus for His burial, and how interesting that she poured out the most expensive perfume she had—worth an entire year's salary—on the most glorious feet ever to walk on the face of this earth or be nailed to an old rugged cross.

2. *Scene of opposites.* A woman demonstrated her love and honor for Jesus. But at the same time His apostles, who also loved Him, criticized and complained (Matthew 26:8). Our Savior knew that His beatings, His trial, His humiliation, and His cross were just hours away, and those closest to Him still did not have a clue as to Jesus' approaching violent and bloody death.

3. *Money was an issue.* All three accounts reveal that His closest followers complained about the cost of the nard—it wasn't only Judas. "Why has this perfume been wasted?" (Mark 14:4). I cannot help but think these words stabbed deeper than a knife into Jesus' soul. What thoughts ran through Your mind, Jesus? Were they thoughts like this: "Have I been with you so long, and you still don't get it?" or "Haven't I shown you how much I love you, and you say these things to me?" or "In a few hours I am going to give up my very life for you. Do you still think this spikenard is being wasted?"

Judas and the other apostles . . . looked at the anointing of Jesus with perfume through different eyes. Mary was looking through the eyes of love. . . . Jesus told the apostles that when the gospel is preached this story will be told. It is being told as one reads and studies this event. It is an inspiration to all. To Jesus it was a great comfort that someone understood to some degree what He was about to go through and expressed her love in a meaningful way. The church needs more Marys.[46]

Mary got the picture when it came to Jesus. She perceived His divinity and His mission. On at least two occasions, Mary followed her heart to learn, listen, and serve. She did not allow any distractions from the surrounding disciples to stop her. I'm convinced that she understood completely what it meant to seek the precious moments with Jesus— something His own apostles did not understand.

The Good Part: She Did What She Could

Jesus always knew what others were thinking, including those of His apostles that evening and of His gracious sister as she anointed His feet so lovingly. He not only experienced her touch and breathed the scent of the precious perfume, He also knew her motivation.

Perhaps that perception of her thoughts prompted Jesus' profound words, "She has done what she could" (Mark 14:8). What can we say after reading those six words? Mary gave what she had and did what she could for our Savior some two thousand years ago, and we still are talking about her. Whoever opens her Bible will know of this event and will be impressed that Jesus honored Mary twice. Once He had said, "Mary has chosen the good part." Later He said, "She has done what she could." Mary's life fascinates us. Mary, I want to meet you some day. You bring tears to my eyes every time I read about you.

On the other hand, reading that same Bible reveals the experiences of a young man named Esau who had no respect for our Father; he had nothing but contempt for Him and His promises. What do you learn from those two hearts? Look at them honestly and openly because God certainly is honest and open in telling us about them.

Your Heart, Your Destiny

The blunt and graphic lesson from Genesis, wrapped up in a privileged person named Esau, jumps right off the pages of the Bible. Furthermore, the ramifications about God and our response to Him are huge. Will we, like Esau, despise God's Law? Will we come to Him weeping when it is too late?

On the other hand, the deeply beautiful and moving lesson from Matthew, Mark, and John reminds us of who we can be for Jesus. Will we, like Mary, understand who Jesus is and seek the precious moments to do all we can for Him? Will we be good daughters, sitting at the feet of the Lord and saying, "Tell me more, Jesus, tell me and teach me more"? Will we find time to take off our shoes because we are on holy ground—in the presence of God? Will we give all we have—our hearts, souls, and minds—to be about our Father's business? What is the sad part of all this? Few there are who really *know* the story of Mary and its depths of love, and few there are who really *know* the story of Esau and his heart of contempt.

Let's resolve today to be one of the few that knows. What is it going to take for us to get into the Word? No truer words were ever spoken than those of our brother Marshall Keeble: "You've got a book and you can take that book and conquer the world, but you can't do it with it under your arm. You've got to have it in your heart."

Oh my sisters, how important it is to find the time for God in our days. Let's respect and honor His marvelous Word, our road map with directions on how to walk with Him. Let's live for Him, die for Him, and live again with Him. No, we may not understand or agree with God in all things, but that is not the point. The point is to be obedient loving children whose greatest desire is to please our Father. How important is it for us to go to heaven? It means everything.

God has a marvelous plan for each of us. Don't give up on it. We must grow our faith, seek His face, and work the plan. Caroline Myss once asked, "Do you really want to look back on your life and see how wonderful it could have been had you not been afraid to live it?" Well, do we?

We must never forget that our Father knows everything there is to know about you and me. He is not fooled. He knows our hearts—something no one else will ever know. God looks down from heaven, searching for a single soul who does right and really seeks Him (Psalm 53:2).

Do you want to have a happy life with God's blessings, my sister? Then surrender to the Master and obey Him with every step that you take. Get to work in His vineyard. I heard Jimmy Judd, a great preacher who spent his life in the mission fields of Malawi, say, "We glorify God when we obey God."

What Time Is It?

What time is it?
Time to do well,
Time to do better,
Give up that grudge,
Answer that letter,
Speak the kind word to
Sweeten a sorrow,
Do that good deed you
Would leave till tomorrow.

—Author unknown

MOMENTS IN PRAYER

Oh Lord, please help me to find the time and take the time and make the time to obey You and glorify Your name. My life is Yours. All that I have is Yours. Show me where I can serve You. May You say to me some day, "Well done, My good and faithful daughter. You have done all you could." In Jesus' name, Amen.

Moments in Song

"Have Thine Own Way, Lord" and "We'll Work Till Jesus Comes"

KEEP SEEKING

1. How many of Esau's relatives can you name?
2. Discuss the references to Mary and Martha in the New Testament.
3. How do you feel when you do something for the Lord?

Timely Quotes

"To be a Christian means to forgive the inexcusable because God has forgiven the inexcusable in you."

—C. S. Lewis

"The church is the great lost and found department."

—Robert Short

"It is impossible to be grateful and hateful at the same time."

—Denzel Washington

Too Late to Say Goodbye

It was the late 1960s when I first met them. They were an older couple at a congregation in Texas where Dad was preaching. We'll call them Ann and Weldon.

Impeccable dressers, they made quite a pair. Both were tall and lithe. They seemed to me to be an easygoing couple, both of them very laid back and soft spoken. They had no children, and it was obvious that they loved one another deeply.

One summer morning they had a spat before Ann left the house for her regular hair appointment. She was upset because he had not mowed the grass. They exchanged a few harsh words, and then she got into her car and headed to town.

Weldon cranked up the lawnmower so he could surprise her when she got home again—all "beautified." He began cutting the grass.

Not too long after this, the phone rang at my parents' home. It was Ann.

"Russ, is that you?" Ann asked.

"Yes, Ann. Are you all right?" Dad replied.

"Russ, can you come over here right now? I just got home from the beauty shop and I think Weldon is hurt. The lawn mower is out and I think he has collapsed in the front yard!" (This was before everyone called 911.)

"I'll be right there."

My dad had been a medic during WWII, and it seemed that everyone turned to him for medical advice. Unlike most kids who run to their mom when they are hurt, the Fowler trio ran to Dad with their hurt fingers, cut toes, splinters, and skinned knees. We did this for one simple reason: Mom always fell apart at any sight of blood, hollering, "Go and get Daddy!"

Dad raced over to Ann and Weldon's home, and as he pulled into the drive, he could see Weldon's long, lanky body lying very still in the ditch on the side of their yard. Dad quickly checked Weldon's pulse and saw that he was gone. He had suffered a heart attack and simply died there. What a sad day that was.

There are times when situations between a married couple do not end well. Not every argument is resolved and ends with peace and kisses. The air is not always cleared. Although as Christians we try to practice "don't let the sun go down upon your wrath" (Ephesians 4:26), there are occasions when invisible miles separate us, and that's just the way it is. I do know that in the marriage relationship, sometimes the best thing is to say nothing and go on living.

Not every couple gets to say goodbye when death comes to them. Weldon and Ann no doubt loved each other, and that was not the way they had planned to say goodbye. If these two had known that this day would be their last day together on earth, what would they have done differently? There would have been more embraces, more kisses, and more loving words between them. Instead, Ann lived the remainder of her life with regret and "if only"—"If only I had said such and such"; "if only I hadn't left the house."

God knew that we would have times when peace between us would be difficult. So He inspired Paul to write, "If possible, so far as it depends on you, be at peace with all men" (Romans 12:18). This passage is probably one of the hardest passages in the Bible to live. But with God's help, anything is possible.

I saw on Pinterest that Augustine, a fourth-century religious philosopher, once aptly said, "Take care of your body as if you were going to live forever, and take care of your soul as if you were going to die today."

Life is too short, my sisters, to dwell on "if only." Love now. Keep the peace now, if possible. Have the guts to say to your loved one, "I am sorry," or at least call and tell them "I'm sorry" when you can. Make the peace with God too. Ask for forgiveness and start over in your walk with Him.

I wonder, why don't we love more like we should? Why don't we love like this is our last day on earth? I think it is because we take life for granted. We soothe ourselves with thoughts of doing things later, and *later* becomes our byword. We think we have all the time in the world to make amends—later. We are imperfect people and imperfect Christians who sometimes have deep regrets. Does that stop us from loving others or even loving God? Oh no. Never! Our love goes on.

So let's do better in this "no regrets" department. Let us resolve to make sure we say "I love you" now to friends and loved ones. Don't be shy. Just say the most wonderful words in the world. Don't hang up the phone without saying them, and don't drive away from a husband or wife or child without letting them know how you feel about them—text the words, if you must.

I never tire of hearing these words. I bet you don't either. It gives me great pleasure to see a grown man talking on a cell phone and saying "I love you" before he hangs up. Here he is, out in public, and he is not ashamed to say what he feels. I absolutely love it.

Let's close this time with a quote from Louise Erdrich:

> Life will break you. Nobody can protect you from that, and living alone won't either, for solitude will also break you with its yearning. You have to love. You have to feel. It is the reason you are here on earth. You are here to risk your heart.

Yes, Ms. Erdrich, you are so right. To not love is to miss out on everything, truly everything. Open up your heart; love your family, love the brethren, love yourself, love the lost, and most of all, love Jesus. Whatever you do, don't be too busy to love. Find the time. You will never regret it.

*Jeff and
Becky Blackmon*

Jesus, Take The Wheel

Well, friends, we are back to the beginning in a way. In chapter 1, we learned, "For I am confident of this very thing, that He who began a good work in you will perfect it until the day of Christ Jesus" (Philippians 1:6). Let's end this book the same way we began, with this powerful passage.

God has begun a magnificent work in our lives, my sisters. Hopefully this book has helped you to see that. What are we doing with the time we have left? Have we considered some ways to reorganize our time and priorities? Have we become wisely built houses? Have we decided to focus on God more and on "things" less? Are we working for the Lord, or are we idle for the Lord? Are we busy using our talents for the Lord, or has Satan taken over our heart? There are so many fabulous scriptures from the mouth of God, urging us to use our talents in His kingdom.

When we became Christians, our lives completely changed. We put away the old self and became a new creature for the Master. We learned to imitate Jesus and do good works everywhere. "You know of Jesus of Nazareth, how God anointed Him with the Holy Spirit and with power, and how He went about doing good and healing all who were oppressed by the devil, for God was with Him" (Acts 10:38).

If Jesus went about doing good, then so should we. If Jesus loved the sinner and not the sin, then so should we. If Jesus answered Satan with "It is written," so should we. Know your Bible. "All Scripture is inspired by God and profitable for teaching, for reproof, for correction, for training in righteousness" (2 Timothy 3:16). Keep reading. Let's look at verse 17: "so that the man of God may be adequate, equipped for every good work."

The Bible teaches us, disciplines us, corrects us, and trains us for right living so that we may be equipped, ready for every good work. The Bible wasn't written by God so we can climb the corporate ladder or acquire great sums of money. The Bible is inspired by God so that you and I have all the elements necessary to do His work.

We sing a hymn that has these lines, "There is much to do; there's work on every hand." And there is much to do. When we are God's children, He is at work in our lives. "For it is God who is at work in you, both to will and to work for His good pleasure" (Philippians 2:13). I think this verse describes us and God as a boomerang: We go out to do God's work, and God sends us back better than when we left. (You have to think about that one.)

Time to Do God's Work

Do we go about doing good like Jesus did? I never think of Jesus shouting, picking fights, and hollering at folks. Instead, I see Him helping a farmer fix his broken cart or holding a child who has fallen and skinned her knee. I see Jesus comforting a woman whose husband has just passed away. And I certainly see Him teaching a group of people about His Father in heaven. These are all good works that we can do too. All we have to do is make the choice to do them.

Jesus made this astounding statement, "And He who sent Me is with Me; He has not left Me alone, for I always do the things that are pleasing to Him" (John 8:29). Can we say that also? Do we always do the things that are pleasing to God? Wow, that passage reaches right down to my soul and shakes me up.

What does God tell us about Dorcas? "This woman was abounding with deeds of kindness and charity which she continually did" (Acts 9:36). Dorcas was a very busy Christian, unfailingly full of wonderful works. Sewing was just one of her many talents.

What about Christians in the early years of the church? Luke tells us of their generosity and loving hearts:

> And the congregation of those who believed were of one heart and soul; and not one of them claimed that anything belonging to him was his own; but all things were common property to them. . . . For there was not a needy person among them, for all who were owners of land or houses would sell them and bring the proceeds of the sales, and lay them at the apostles' feet; and they would be distributed to each as any had need (Acts 4:32, 34–35).

Paul speaks to all Christians today with these words to Timothy: "Instruct them to do good, to be rich in good works, to be generous and ready to share" (1 Timothy 6:18). Note that Paul urges those who are rich in this chapter—and we are rich!—to focus on being rich in good works and not to be poor in good works. Think about that.

Paul also called attention to the Macedonian churches and their generosity by saying, "but they first gave themselves to the Lord" (2 Corinthians 8:5). Oh, that this could be said about all of us, every congregation of the Lord's body, that we gave ourselves first to the Lord. The Lord must always be first—never anything or anyone else.

Pause and Ponder

Memorize 1 Timothy 6:18 and focus on putting it into practice. How can we be poor in good works?

Moments That Matter

Jane McWhorter was a wonderful Christian woman, wife, mother, teacher, author, and friend. I am happy to say that I knew her. There was nobody like Jane, no one more humble and no one more encouraging. Jane loved the Lord and was an excellent Bible student. I encourage you to read her book, *She Hath Done What She Could*. Since we are talking about doing good works here, let's see what Jane wrote concerning this matter:

> Service to others assumes a deeper significance when we realize this: Serving others is the only way we can minister to Christ because He is not physically present. Notice Matthew's comment at the crucifixion: "And many women who followed Jesus from Galilee, ministering to Him, were looking on from afar" (Matthew 27:55).
>
> How gladly we would have cared for His needs had we been there, yet He tells us that we serve Him by serving others. "Inasmuch as you did it to one of the least of these, My brethren, you did it to Me" (Matthew 25:40).[47]

I love these thoughts because too often we do forget why we do what we do for the Lord. We are told to do good works and we desire to be like Jesus as He "went about doing good." But we forget that when we help another, we are helping Jesus. When we take food to others, we are feeding Jesus. When we provide rest, comfort, or shelter, it is Jesus we are serving. Nothing else matters.

Our congregation receives *Power for Today*, a small booklet with a message for every day of the year, written by Christians all over America and published by 21st Century Christian Foundation. It is jam packed full of treasures, and several years ago I found wisdom in this remark by Eddie Lewis: "Sometimes we feel we must do some great work to be successful in God's eyes, but God wants us first to do the work where we are!"

Isn't this true? Don't we feel that we have to do something mighty and huge and fantabulous to merit any favor from God? And all along, the only thing He ever wants is for us to work right where He has planted us. Sometimes we are hesitant, not knowing where we fit. What talents do we have? Consider these wise words.

> We can't all go to Africa or China. But we can help one person—one neighbor or friend or missionary. We can bloom where we are planted. . . . Too often, we do nothing while we wait for the opportunity to do something big.
>
> Use the talent you have, no matter how small it may seem. Use the tools you have at hand. Can you cook? Sign up to help with the fellowship meals. Take food to those who have been in the hospital, the bereaved, the new neighbor, or even an old neighbor. Get to know the people who enjoy your pies or cakes, then invite them to church or offer to study with them.
>
> Do you like to talk? Visit the shut-ins and the sick; encourage them with kind words; read scripture and pray with them. Maybe you don't like to talk or can't get out much yourself. Do you have paper and a pen? Envelopes and stamps? Write to those who are sick or bereaved. Write to the teen-agers or the preacher or the elders and tell them you are praying for them. Write to new converts and include a list of Bible verses to encourage them. Become involved with World Bible School and mail correspondence courses to people who have never heard of Jesus.
>
> The possibilities are endless; God gave you at least one talent.[48]

Time to Be a Barnabas

Throughout this book, I have been writing about doing and working for the Lord, so now it's time for each of us to be a Barnabas. Imagine how much the early church needed encouragement and comfort. Barnabas was a godsend—literally.

When we read the book of Acts, we can easily grasp how much this early Christian was loved and treasured for his encouraging ways. To begin with, his name wasn't even Barnabas, it was Joseph. But the apostles in Jerusalem had renamed him Barnabas because that name meant "son of encouragement" (Acts 4:36)—and that name described him perfectly.

It is Barnabas who courageously defends Saul when Saul comes to Jerusalem (Acts 9). It is Barnabas that the Jerusalem church trusts to send off to Antioch to check on the work there and to encourage all the Christians to remain true. He is even entrusted with monies to carry back to Jerusalem for the famine to come (Acts 11). It is also Barnabas who travels with Paul on his first missionary journey, encouraging the brethren, teaching and establishing congregations. When we get to heaven, it will be terrific to meet our brother from Cyprus.

The early church needed a whole lot of boosting and approval, and God selected Barnabas for the job. Girls, may we never forget that God is in the "Blessing Business," and He blesses us with unusual people who make it their business to encourage us. God sends people who possess the talent for a specific work He has in mind. Remember He knows just what we need. Get ready, my sister, because God will use you to help someone else. There is no higher honor than to be used by God and for God.

My sister Brenda in Florida is one of the best encouragers that I know. She is a five-foot-tall powerhouse! I think of her as a cheerleader without pompoms. God surely put her on this planet to search out brothers and sisters who need to hear good and kind words. And that's what she does. She makes it her business to lift up everyone in the family of God. She once told me, "Every worship service is a chance to encourage someone." She is right, isn't she? Just think of all those missed opportunities when we didn't do some of that encouraging ourselves. Why can't we be cheerleaders too?

I don't care how old we are or how mature in the faith we are, we all need to be encouraged and patted on the back. A preacher once summarized it this way, "We have to help keep the strong, strong, so they can help the weak and struggling."

Encouragement is a much-needed ministry. Remember, to be a ministry, it must be consistent. It cannot be something that you hit-and-miss once in a while when you feel like it. It is a great ministry, but will require your time and planning. . . . It is best to have a certain day, or time of day, that you plan to devote to this ministry. Monday morning is a great time to sit down with your church bulletin and announcements . . . and write your notes of encouragement. Encouragement givers can open doors for the gospel that no one else has managed to do. Is this your ministry?"[49]

I challenge you from this day on to be a Barnabas in your congregation. Like Zacchaeus who was on the lookout for Jesus, start looking out for the newcomer, the one who has walked into the church building all alone and does not know a soul. Walk up to her. Smile. Remember that God is with you. Keep in mind how it feels to be a visitor who is sensitive and feeling awkward. Invite her to come and sit with you. I cannot tell you how many times I have seen the most grateful expressions in visitors' eyes when they are welcomed that way.

Encourage the men who take part in the worship, and thank them for their volunteer spirit. Pray for the elders. Send them notes of support as they care for the flock. Hug the children and tell them you love them. Stop and talk to the older people who have little family. Hug them too, for they do not get much affection. Tell the young men you are thankful for them as they lead prayers, songs, and serve at the Lord's table. Encourage the girls as they serve the women in songs, prayers, and spiritual talks. Everybody needs encouraging words, and everybody needs to feel the love of the family. Open your heart, my sister, and give, give, give.

Do not discourage our precious family. How careful we must be with our words so as not to hurt anyone. I'm reminded of this true but sad event.

My mother once witnessed a nervous young man, easily embarrassed, who was appointed to close worship with prayer. Very shakily he walked to the microphone and led the congregation as best he could.

Immediately afterwards an older woman approached and remarked, "Young man, if I couldn't pray better than that, I wouldn't pray at all!" Can you guess what happened? That young man never led another public prayer. Perhaps he never returned to worship. God is not pleased when we sit in critical judgment of leaders who are doing their best. The attitude of one's heart is God's business, not ours.[50]

May we always keep this verse in our hearts, "Let us consider how to stimulate one another to love and good deeds" (Hebrews 10:24).

Time-Out from the Comfort Zone

Be a Barnabas wherever you go. Smile, look people in the eye, and tell them, "God is good!" or "Have a blessed day!" Our church has cards that we can pass out to invite people to our services. We leave them in restaurants and doctor and dentist offices. I give them to the repairmen who come to my home and invite them to come to church and sit with me. I have never had anyone refuse a card. And if I see this fellow's toolbox, I put another card there too, because that repairman just might lose the first card I gave him. I could go on and on, but you understand what I am saying. Staying in your comfort zone is not always wise. Karen Salmansohn once wrote, "A comfort zone is a beautiful place, but nothing ever grows there." Amen!

Let's be easy to love, not difficult. A billboard once proclaimed: "Want to be loved? Be lovable!" Girls, we are Jesus' sisters, and we reflect His light. Look how many followed Him wherever He went. He was lovable, and people felt comfortable with Him. Find the time to be someone's blessing everywhere you go.

Pause and Ponder

Look up the following passages from Psalms and see what David wrote in the Old Testament about serving God: Psalms 34:13; 37:3; and 37:27. How do these verses apply to the benefits of encouragement?

Paul wrote these words to the church at Ephesus which was being bombarded with all kinds of error, "Therefore be careful how you walk, not as unwise men but as wise, making the most of your time [redeeming the time], because the days are evil" (Ephesians 5:15–16).

Yes, the days are evil, and yet God still allows the world to keep on revolving. As I am typing this passage from Ephesians, I see that Paul urges the church to "be careful how you walk." Girls, every step we take as a Christian should be right beside our Lord Jesus Christ. Don't we want to walk with Him, making the most of our time? We've got to use our precious time—not waste it.

All we have is today. The Hebrews writer knew it well when he wrote, "But encourage one another day after day, as long as it is still called 'Today,' so that none of you will be hardened by the deceitfulness of sin" (Hebrews 3:13).

Excuses, Excuses

There is nothing new under the sun when it comes to people and excuses. When Jesus was here on earth, not everyone embraced His call for them to follow Him. The following passage clearly reveals that when Jesus called some people personally, they told Him that they could not follow Him—right then. They had the "later" mentality.

> And He said to another, "Follow Me." But he said, "Lord, permit me first to go and bury my father." But He said to him, "Allow the dead to bury their own dead; but as for you, go and proclaim everywhere the kingdom of God." Another also said, "I will follow You, Lord; but first permit me to say good-bye to those at home." But Jesus said to him, "No one, after putting his hand to the plow and looking back, is fit for the kingdom of God (Luke 9:59–62).

In another parable Jesus told about the slighted invitation, the one where a host (God) invited many to a big dinner. All kinds of excuses came forth: a man was busy with real estate; another man purchased oxen (a business deal), and one man was just married (family relations). In reality, all these men were saying, "I just don't have the time."

Pause and Ponder

Read Luke 14:16–24 in your Bible and circle the excuses.

Felix, the governor of Judea, stands out as verbalizing the "excuse of all excuses." He said the same thing many people say in their hearts when they refuse to deal with their sin problems. As Paul stood before Felix and his young wife Drusilla, he preached the best gospel sermon ever. Instead of begging for his own life, Paul preached the truth of Jesus, hoping that Felix and Drusilla would be saved. Luke records that Paul's lesson even scared Felix. Let's look at that day in Caesarea.

> But some days later Felix arrived with Drusilla, his wife who was a Jewess, and sent for Paul and heard him speak about faith in Christ Jesus. But as he was discussing righteousness, self-control and the judgment to come, Felix became frightened and said, "Go away for the present, and when I find time I will summon you" (Acts 24:24–25).

"When I find time." Haven't we all heard those words? Felix couldn't handle the truth because he had no desire to change his life. Evidently Felix never found time to become a Christian. And neither did Drusilla. Some twenty years later, she perished with their son in the volcanic ash of Pompeii.

Almost Persuaded

There are all kinds of excuses people give for not meeting God, for not loving God, and for not obeying God. I have heard many, and I imagine you have too.

The following was an actual event that took place in a Texas farming community. There was a small church of Christ in this town. Every preacher who moved into that community made it his aim to convert a certain farmer who attended with his wife. Years passed, preachers came and went, but the farmer never responded to the invitation of the Lord.

One day the farmer was seriously injured in a tractor accident. Two men who witnessed the accident ran to the farmer, picked him up, put him into their car, and rushed him to the hospital.

As they approached that little church the farmer attended, he begged them to stop and let the preacher baptize him. However, the men felt the hospital was more important, so they sped past it toward the emergency room. The fatally injured man died at the hospital that day, saying, "But I always *meant* to become a Christian."

There are many things we mean to do in this life. We will get around to them one of these days, or will we? No, we often put off and put off until it is too late. We recklessly and foolishly think we have all the time in the world. What is so tragic is that our soul is at stake, and how much is that worth? And one of these days, girls, our time will be up! I cannot help but think of that hymn from long ago, "Almost Persuaded"—"almost, but lost." Why oh why would any of us play Russian roulette with our soul?

Paul encouraged the Philippians with these words, "One thing I do: forgetting what lies behind [the past] and reaching forward to what lies ahead [the future], I press on [present] toward the goal for the prize of the upward call of God in Christ Jesus" (Philippians 3:13–14).

So my sweet sisters, we are forgetting about the past, looking toward the future, but always pressing on to the work at hand. Today is all we have. Mama penned these words:

> How much time do we have left? When is the trumpet going to blow? God tells us to "redeem the time," or buy it up. Many reason within themselves, "When we get this house paid for, then we will begin to live." Or "when the kids get in school or out of school, then things will be different, more orderly."
>
> I remember asking a dear friend of mine why older people did not start living closer to God because they had to know that they were getting close to death. She answered wisely, "We die like we live."

Too many of us intend to try it God's way some day but not now. We put a distant goal in our minds when we will change and become more godly, but time cannot be counted on.[51]

Now Is the Time

My precious sisters, these are our precious moments, and they are quickly vanishing. Our lives are like a vapor, and the hands of time are whizzing around the clock we call Life. "For we are only of yesterday and know nothing, because our days on earth are as a shadow" (Job 8:9).

Now is our moment. There is no dress rehearsal for this life. We are on stage, the play has begun, and some of us are in the final act. What does our God want from us? He simply wants us.

Living for God is our highest calling. We do not have a long time, so let's do all we can while we can. Surely with the good minds that God has given us, we can figure out how to put the latest novel down and pick up God's word. How hard is it to organize our daily life in such a way that we can take the time for reading our Bible, for studying our lessons, or for prayer? Let's make the Father our top priority each day. Isn't it still true that we find the time to do the things we really want to do?

Jesus so wisely warned us two thousand years ago, "We must work the works of Him who sent Me as long as it is day; night is coming when no one can work" (John 9:4). So let's get to work. One of these days our Savior is coming back, and there will be a Judgment Day. Will we be ready? Will we run to meet Jesus or will we try to run and hide?

I especially love these valuable thoughts:

God created woman with a heart for loving, a mind for learning, and hands for giving, and woman should, in return, desire to grow in the ability to use these attributes in God's service. Christ's great commandment (Mark 12:30) encompasses all. The Christian woman responds to this commandment by saying, "All that I am, all that I have, all that I hope to be, I dedicate to You."[52]

Let's look at what God inspired Paul to write from prison:

For this reason also, since the day we heard of it, we have not ceased to pray for you and to ask that you may be *filled* with the knowledge of His will in all spiritual wisdom and understanding, so that you will *walk* in a manner worthy of the Lord, to *please* Him in all respects, *bearing fruit* in every good work and *increasing* in the knowledge of God; *strengthened* with all power, according to His glorious might, for the attaining of all steadfastness and patience; joyously *giving thanks* to the Father, who has qualified us to share in the inheritance of the saints in Light (Colossians 1:9–12, emphasis mine).

What a wonderful verse for bottom-line Christian living. Notice the words I emphasized. God wants us filled with knowledge, walking worthily, pleasing Him, bearing fruit, increasing in more knowledge, strengthened with power, and giving thanks joyously. This is the life of every Christian. To miss out on it would be the biggest tragedy ever. It is the only way to live.

Pause and Ponder

Isolate each action of Colossians 1:9–12 on separate index cards. Rotate the cards each day for a month, focusing on one card per day.

W. Tozer said, "If God gives you a few more years, remember, it is not yours. Your time must honor God, your activity must honor God, and everything you do must honor God." Solomon wrote in Ecclesiastes 9:10: "Whatever your hand finds to do, verily, do it with all your might." Paul said it this way in Colossians 3:17: "Whatever you do in word or deed, do all in the name of the Lord Jesus, giving thanks through Him to God the Father." Do how much? All—everything.

God reminds us about the brevity of our lives and stresses the importance of putting on Christ. Listen to His admonition written by Paul:

Do this, knowing the time, that it is already the hour for you to awaken from sleep; for now salvation is nearer to us than when we believed. The night is almost gone, and the day is near. Therefore let us lay aside the deeds of darkness and put on the armor of light. Let us behave properly as in the day, not in carousing and drunkenness, not in sexual promiscuity and sensuality, not in strife and jealousy. But put on the Lord Jesus Christ, and make no provision for the flesh in regard to its lusts (Romans 13:11–14).

It Is Time to Go

Well, my precious sisters, to the work! Let's go. Today is the day, for tomorrow never comes. We are not Scarlett O'Hara, vowing to "think about that tomorrow." This is our moment, and the time is now.

The Holy Spirit inspired Paul to tell the church at Corinth, "'At the acceptable time I listened to you, and on the day of salvation I helped you.' Behold, now is 'the acceptable time,' behold, now is 'the day of salvation'" (2 Corinthians 6:2).

The precious moment is now, so let's get busy letting our lights shine and reflecting our Savior. God, the Creator of time, will one day end time just as easily as it began. He will stop all clocks and say, "Time is no more." As my little Mama used to say, "Remember, Becky, there is a day fixed" (Acts 17:31). That will be a glorious day!

Our kind and merciful Jesus beckons to each one of us and pleads, "Come and follow Me." Will we hear His call or reject His call? What excuses will we give? Remember, Jesus once said, "No one, after putting his hand to the plow and looking back, is fit for the kingdom of God" (Luke 9:62). The Greek word for "fit" here means useful or well placed. I want to be fit, useful and well placed for the kingdom of God. I am not putting my hand to the plow and looking back, my sisters. I want God to know that He can always depend on me. I am in this Christian life for keeps. No turning back. I'll follow Him.

So in the meantime, let us say like little Samuel, "Here I am, Lord. Your servant is listening." And, let us be a woman like the mighty messianic prophet Isaiah, and say, "Here am I, Lord. Send me!"

At the End of the Day

You know what all of this is all about, don't you? It's called love. We find the time for the things we love. If we don't love God, we will never find the time for Him, anywhere or anytime. And the opposite is true. When we love God, we will always find the time for Him, because He is number one with us—at the top of the list. Nothing can take His place. He is God and there is no other.

I love you, my precious sisters. I am praying for you daily. We all want to go to heaven, don't we? Then let's find the time for God, Jesus, and the Holy Spirit who tell us how to get there. Let's live that life of a lifetime God has so graciously given each of us. Let's make His time our time. What on earth is more important than our precious God?

Remember, I will meet you at the gate—heaven's gate. God bless you. I sure do love you with all my heart.

Love,

Becky

The Clock of Life

The clock of life is wound but once,
And no man has the power
To tell just when the hands will stop
At late or early hour.

To lose one's wealth is sad indeed,
To lose one's health is more,
To lose one's soul is such a loss
That no man can restore.

The present only is our own,
So live, love, toil with a will,
Place no faith in "Tomorrow,"
For the Clock may then be still."

—Robert H. Smith[53]

MOMENTS IN PRAYER

Oh precious Father, we bow down at Your feet. You are our God, and we are Your children. We love You with all of our being. Thank You for the blessings You pour down upon our heads. How can we ever possibly thank You enough for Jesus? Thank You for forgiving us of our sins, and thank You for the promise of heaven. Thank You for the Holy Spirit who gave us Your Word in the Bible, and we thank You, Father, for You. Please, please don't give up on us. And Lord, please help us find the time to be about Your business, like Your Son was. We love You, we live for You, and we shall never stop loving You. In Jesus' name, Amen.

Moments in Song

"Sing the Wondrous Love of Jesus" and "Almost Persuaded"

KEEP SEEKING

1. What is the first thing that pops into your head that you can do for the Lord today?
2. Discuss the importance of walking with and pleasing the Lord.
3. What can you do to be a Barnabas in your congregation?

 Timely Quotes

"Don't wait for things to get better. Life will always be complicated. Learn to be happy right now, otherwise you'll run out of time."

—Anonymous

"We don't owe the world an apology because we have the Truth; we owe the world the Truth."

—Lisa Ripperton

"Time is what we want most, but . . . what we use worst."

—William Penn

THE TRAIN OF LIFE

At birth we boarded the train and met our parents, and we believe they will always travel by our side. As time goes by, other people will board the train; and they will be significant—i.e. our siblings, friends, children, and even the love of our life. However, at some station our parents will step down from the train, leaving us on this journey alone. Others will step down over time and leave a permanent vacuum. Some, however, will go so unnoticed that we don't realize they vacated their seats. This train ride will be full of joy, sorrow, fantasy, expectations, hellos, goodbyes, and farewells. Success consists of having a good relationship with all passengers requiring that we give the best of ourselves.

The mystery to everyone is: we do not know at which station we ourselves will step down. So, we must live in the best way, love, forgive, and offer the best of who we are. It is important to do this because when the time comes for us to step down and leave our seat empty, we should leave behind beautiful memories for those who will continue to travel on the train of life. I wish you all a joyful journey.

—Unknown

Endnotes

1. Becky Blackmon, *The Begging Place* (Huntsville, Ala.: Publishing Designs, Inc., 2006), p. 100.

2. Charles Keith King, "Godly Women," *Power for Today* (Nashville: 20th Century Christian Foundation).

3. *Coffman Commentaries on the Old and New Testament*, Matthew 25:24, https://www.studylight.org/commentaries/bcc/matthew-25.html.

4. Author Unknown, "The Beginning of a New Day," http://www.appleseeds.org /Beginning-New-Day.htm.

5. Matthew Henry, *Matthew Henry's Concise Commentary*, John 14, studylight.org.

6. *Coffman Commentaries on the Old and New Testament*, Psalm 139:16, http://classic .studylight.org/com/bcc/view.cgi?book=ps&chapter=139.

7. *Coffman Commentaries on the Old and New Testament*, Ephesians 1:4, https://www .studylight.org/commentaries/bcc/ephesians-1.html.

8. *Coffman Commentaries on the Old and New Testament*, Galatians 4:4, https://www .studylight.org/commentaries/bcc/galatians-4.html.

9. The Nelson Study Bible, NKJV (Nashville, Tenn: Thomas Nelson, Inc., 1997).

10. Wayne Jackson, *New Testament Commentary* (Jackson, Tenn.: Christian Courier Publications, 2011), p. 375.

11. Les Christie, "America's Homes Are Getting Even Bigger," CNN Money (June 5, 2014). https://money.cnn.com/2014/06/04/real_estate/american-home-size/index .html. Accessed Nov. 11, 2018.

12. The Nelson Study Bible, NKJV (Nashville, Tenn: Thomas Nelson, Inc., 1997).

13. *Coffman Commentaries on the Old and New Testament*, Psalm 127, http://classic .studylight.org/com/bcc/view.cgi?book=ps&chapter=127.

14. *Coffman Commentaries on the Old and New Testament*, Luke 6:47, https://www .studylight.org/commentaries/bcc/luke-6.html.

15. *Matthew Henry's Concise Commentary on the Bible*, Proverbs 24:3–6, https://www .studylight.org/commentaries/mhn/proverbs-24.html.

16. Becky Blackmon, *The Begging Place* (Huntsville, Ala.: Publishing Designs Inc., 2006), pp. 38–39.

17. Jane McWhorter, *Roses in December* (Huntsville, Ala.: Publishing Designs, Inc., 2007), p. 132.

18. Rosemary McKnight, *Those Who Wait* (Nashville, Tenn.: Gospel Advocate, 1989), pp. 26–27.

19. James Burton Coffman, *Commentary on Galatians, Ephesians, Philippians, Colossians* (Abilene, Texas: ACU Press, 1977), p. 304.

20. Frank Chesser, *Voyage of Faith* (Huntsville, Ala.: Publishing Designs, Inc., 2010), p. 145.

21. Author Unknown, *Satan's Worldwide Convention*, http://epistle.us/inspiration/satanconvention.html.

22. *Coffman Commentaries on the Old and New Testament*, Luke 15:8, https://www.studylight.org/commentaries/bcc/luke-15.html.

23. Wayne Jackson, *New Testament Commentary* (Jackson, Tenn.: Christian Courier Publications, 2011), p. 118.

24. *Adam Clarke Commentary*, Luke 15:8, https://www.studylight.org/commentaries/acc/luke-15.html.

25. *Coffman Commentaries on the Old and New Testament*, John 2:14, https://www.studylight.org/commentaries/bcc/john-2.html.

26. Frank Chesser, *Voyage of Faith* (Huntsville, Ala.: Publishing Designs, Inc., 2010), p. 147.

27. John Wilbur Chapman, *1001 Quotations That Connect* (Grand Rapids, Mich.: Zondervan, 2009), p. 10.

28. *Coffman Commentaries on the Old and New Testament*, Philippians 4:8, https://www.studylight.org/commentaries/bcc/philippians-4.html.

29. Jim Sheerer, *New Testament Commentary* (Walton, Kan.: Yeoman Press LLC, 2001), p. 317.

30. Becky Blackmon, *The Begging Place* (Huntsville, Ala.: Publishing Designs, Inc., 2006), p. 127.

31. Jane McWhorter, *She Hath Done What She Could* (Huntsville, Ala.: Publishing Designs, Inc., 2015), p. 37.

32. Adam Faughn, *A Legacy of Faith* blog, http://www.faughnfamily.com. Used by permission.

33. Kathy McWhorter Kendall, *Becoming a Woman God Can Use* (Huntsville, Ala.: Publishing Designs, Inc., 2017), pp. 120–121.

34. *Coffman Commentaries on the Old and New Testament*, Matthew 11:28, https://www.studylight.org/commentaries/bcc/matthew-11.html.

35. Ronald D. Lesley, "Facts from History About Our King James Bible: The Manuscript Period," http://www.fbinstitute.com/engbible/4.html.

36. Wayne Jackson, *New Testament Commentary* (Jackson, Tenn.: Christian Courier Publications, 2011), p. 59.

37. Jane McWhorter, *Roses in December* (Huntsville, Ala.: Publishing Designs, Inc., 2007), p. 161.

38. Adam Faughn, *A Legacy of Faith* blog, http://www.faughnfamily.com. Used by permission.

39. Mahita Gajanan, "The Cost of Raising a Child Jumps to $233,610," Time.com, Jan. 9, 2017. http://time.com/money/4629700/child-raising-cost-department-of -agriculture-report.

40. Bill Tinsley, "Religion: Stories That Save Us; Bible's Heritage, Lessons Being Lost," *Waco Tribune-Herald*, July 30, 2016. https://www.wacotrib.com /news/religion/religion-stories-that-save-us-bible-s-heritage-lessons-being /article_4e9a1d92-da66-587e-950d-922b176ce3a2.html.

41. Frank Chesser, *Voyage of Faith* (Huntsville, Ala.: Publishing Designs, Inc., 2010), pp. 140–141.

42. Author Unknown, "Back Home." https://ryanvandeput.wordpress.com/2015/09 /03/heres-a-poem-called-back-home-by-an-unknown.

43. *Coffman Commentaries on the Old and New Testament*, Hebrews 12:16–17, https:// www.studylight.org/commentaries/bcc/hebrews-12.html.

44. Jason Jackson, "Too Late for Tears." ChristianCourier.com. Access date: June 19, 2018. https://www.christiancourier.com/articles/1242-too-late-for-tears.

45. *Coffman Commentaries on the Old and New Testament*, Matthew 26:6, https:// www.studylight.org/commentaries/bcc/matthew-26.html.

46. Jim Sheerer, *New Testament Commentary* (Walton, Kan.: Yeoman Press LLC, 2001), p. 216.

47. Jane McWhorter, *She Hath Done What She Could* (Huntsville, Ala.: Publishing Designs, Inc., 2015), p. 16.

48. Deborah Mitchell, *First Sisters* (Winona, Miss.: J. C. Choate Publications, 2008), pp. 44–45.

49. Pam Stewart, *Evangelistic Women* (Kearney, Neb.: Morris Publishing, 2000), pp. 124–125.

50. Becky Blackmon, *The Begging Place* (Huntsville, Ala.: Publishing Designs, Inc., 2006), p. 160.

51. Lea Fowler, *Precious Are God's Plans* (Quality Publications, 1986), pp. 123–124.

52. Irene Young Mattox, *Patterns for Living* (Nashville, Tenn.: 20th Century Christian, 1971).

53. Robert H. Smith, "The Clock of Life," goodreads.com.

SOURCES

AZQuotes.com   Goodreads.com   Pinterest
Brainyquote.com   JustLifeQuotes

CPSIA information can be obtained
at www.ICGtesting.com
Printed in the USA
LVHW082213300721
693607LV00004B/4